Interactions 1

LISTENING/SPEAKING

Judith Tanka

Paul Most

Jami Hanreddy
Listening/Speaking Strand Leader

Interactions 1 Listening/Speaking, Silver Edition

ISBN 13: 978-0-07-333742-5 (Student Book with Audio Highlights)
ISBN 10: 0-07-333742-0
5 6 7 8 9 10 VNH 11 10 09

Editorial director: Erik Gundersen
Series editor: Valerie Kelemen
Developmental editor: Mari Vargo
Production manager: Juanita Thompson
Production coordinator: Vanessa Nuttry
Cover designer: Robin Locke Monda
Interior designer: Nesbitt Graphics, Inc.
Artists: Burgandy Beam, Chris Dyrud, Kay McCabe, NETS, Laura Nikiel, Linda Bittner, Jonathan Massie, Allan & Deborah Drew-Brook-Cormack
Photo researcher: Photoquick Research

The credits section for this book begins on page iv and is considered an extension of the copyright page.

Cover photo: Steve Allen/Creatas Images

www.esl-elt.mcgraw-hill.com

The McGraw·Hill Companies

A Special Thank You

The Interactions/Mosaic Silver Edition team wishes to thank our extended team: teachers, students, administrators, and teacher trainers, all of whom contributed invaluably to the making of this edition.

Macarena Aguilar, **North Harris College**, Houston, Texas ■ Mohamad Al-Alam, **Imam Mohammad University**, Riyadh, Saudi Arabia ■ Faisal M. Al Mohanna Abaalkhail, **King Saud University**, Riyadh, Saudi Arabia; Amal Al-Toaimy, **Women's College, Prince Sultan University**, Riyadh, Saudi Arabia ■ Douglas Arroliga, **Ave Maria University**, Managua, Nicaragua ■ Fairlie Atkinson, **Sungkyunkwan University**, Seoul, Korea ■ Jose R. Bahamonde, **Miami-Dade Community College**, Miami, Florida ■ John Ball, **Universidad de las Americas**, Mexico City, Mexico ■ Steven Bell, **Universidad la Salle**, Mexico City, Mexico ■ Damian Benstead, **Sungkyunkwan University**, Seoul, Korea ■ Paul Cameron, **National Chengchi University**, Taipei, Taiwan R.O.C. ■ Sun Chang, **Soongsil University**, Seoul, Korea ■ Grace Chao, **Soochow University**, Taipei, Taiwan R.O.C. ■ Chien Ping Chen, **Hua Fan University**, Taipei, Taiwan R.O.C. ■ Selma Chen, **Chihlee Institute of Technology**, Taipei, Taiwan R.O.C. ■ Sylvia Chiu, **Soochow University**, Taipei, Taiwan R.O.C. ■ Mary Colonna, **Columbia University**, New York, New York ■ Lee Culver, **Miami-Dade Community College**, Miami, Florida ■ Joy Durighello, **City College of San Francisco**, San Francisco, California ■ Isabel Del Valle, **Ulatina**, San Jose, Costa Rica ■ Linda Emerson, **Sogang University**, Seoul, Korea ■ Esther Entin, **Miami-Dade Community College**, Miami, Florida ■ Glenn Farrier, **Gakushuin Women's College**, Tokyo, Japan ■ Su Wei Feng, **Taipei**, Taiwan R.O.C. ■ Judith Garcia, **Miami-Dade Community College**, Miami, Florida ■ Maxine Gillway, **United Arab Emirates University**, Al Ain, United Arab Emirates ■ Colin Gullberg, **Soochow University**, Taipei, Taiwan R.O.C. ■ Natasha Haugnes, **Academy of Art University**, San Francisco, California ■ Barbara Hockman, **City College of San Francisco**, San Francisco, California ■ Jinyoung Hong, **Sogang University**, Seoul, Korea ■ Sherry Hsieh, **Christ's College**, Taipei, Taiwan R.O.C. ■ Yu-shen Hsu, **Soochow University**, Taipei, Taiwan R.O.C. ■ Cheung Kai-Chong, **Shih-Shin University**, Taipei, Taiwan R.O.C. ■ Leslie Kanberg, **City College of San Francisco**, San Francisco, California ■ Gregory Keech, **City College of San Francisco**, San Francisco, California ■ Susan Kelly, **Sogang University**, Seoul, Korea ■ Myoungsuk Kim, **Soongsil University**, Seoul, Korea ■ Youngsuk Kim, **Soongsil University**, Seoul, Korea ■ Roy Langdon, **Sungkyunkwan University**, Seoul, Korea ■ Rocio Lara, **University of Costa Rica**, San Jose, Costa Rica ■ Insung Lee, **Soongsil University**, Seoul, Korea ■ Andy Leung, **National Tsing Hua University**, Taipei, Taiwan R.O.C. ■ Elisa Li Chan, **University of Costa Rica**, San Jose, Costa Rica ■ Elizabeth Lorenzo, **Universidad Internacional de las Americas**, San Jose, Costa Rica ■

Cheryl Magnant, **Sungkyunkwan University**, Seoul, Korea ■ Narciso Maldonado Iuit, **Escuela Tecnica Electricista**, Mexico City, Mexico ■ Shaun Manning, **Hankuk University of Foreign Studies**, Seoul, Korea ■ Yoshiko Matsubayashi, **Tokyo International University**, Saitama, Japan ■ Scott Miles, **Sogang University**, Seoul, Korea ■ William Mooney, **Chinese Culture University**, Taipei, Taiwan R.O.C. ■ Jeff Moore, **Sungkyunkwan University**, Seoul, Korea ■ Mavelin de Moreno, **Lehnsen Roosevelt School**, Guatemala City, Guatemala ■ Ahmed Motala, **University of Sharjah, Sharjah**, United Arab Emirates ■ Carlos Navarro, **University of Costa Rica**, San Jose, Costa Rica ■ Dan Neal, **Chih Chien University**, Taipei, Taiwan R.O.C. ■ Margarita Novo, **University of Costa Rica**, San Jose, Costa Rica ■ Karen O'Neill, **San Jose State University**, San Jose, California ■ Linda O'Roke, **City College of San Francisco**, San Francisco, California ■ Martha Padilla, **Colegio de Bachilleres de Sinaloa**, Culiacan, Mexico ■ Allen Quesada, **University of Costa Rica**, San Jose, Costa Rica ■ Jim Rogge, **Broward Community College**, Ft. Lauderdale, Florida ■ Marge Ryder, **City College of San Francisco**, San Francisco, California ■ Gerardo Salas, **University of Costa Rica**, San Jose, Costa Rica ■ Shigeo Sato, **Tamagawa University**, Tokyo, Japan ■ Lynn Schneider, **City College of San Francisco**, San Francisco, California ■ Devan Scoble, **Sungkyunkwan University**, Seoul, Korea ■ Maryjane Scott, **Soongsil University**, Seoul, Korea ■ Ghaida Shaban, **Makassed Philanthropic School**, Beirut, Lebanon ■ Maha Shalok, **Makassed Philanthropic School**, Beirut, Lebanon ■ John Shannon, **University of Sharjah**, Sharjah, United Arab Emirates ■ Elsa Sheng, **National Technology College of Taipei**, Taipei, Taiwan R.O.C. ■ Ye-Wei Sheng, **National Taipei College of Business**, Taipei, Taiwan R.O.C. ■ Emilia Sobaja, **University of Costa Rica**, San Jose, Costa Rica ■ You-Souk Yoon, **Sungkyunkwan University**, Seoul, Korea ■ Shanda Stromfield, **San Jose State University**, San Jose, California ■ Richard Swingle, **Kansai Gaidai College**, Osaka, Japan ■ Carol Sung, **Christ's College, Taipei**, Taiwan R.O.C. ■ Jeng-Yih Tim Hsu, **National Kaohsiung First University of Science and Technology**, Kaohsiung, Taiwan R.O.C. ■ Shinichiro Torikai, **Rikkyo University**, Tokyo, Japan ■ Sungsoon Wang, **Sogang University**, Seoul, Korea ■ Kathleen Wolf, **City College of San Francisco**, San Francisco, California ■ Sean Wray, **Waseda University International**, Tokyo, Japan ■ Belinda Yanda, **Academy of Art University**, San Francisco, California ■ Su Huei Yang, **National Taipei College of Business**, Taipei, Taiwan R.O.C. ■ Tzu Yun Yu, **Chungyu Institute of Technology**, Taipei, Taiwan R.O.C.

Author Acknowledgements

Dedicated to my family, friends and to my students around the world.
—Judith Tanka

Photo Credits

Table of Contents

Welcome to Interactions/Mosaic Silver Edition

Interactions/Mosaic Silver Edition is a fully-integrated, 18-book academic skills series. Language proficiencies are articulated from the beginning through advanced levels <u>within</u> each of the four language skill strands. Chapter themes articulate <u>across</u> the four skill strands to systematically recycle content, vocabulary, and grammar.

NEW to the Silver Edition:

- **World's most popular and comprehensive academic skills series**—thoroughly updated for today's global learners
- **Full-color design** showcases compelling instructional photos to strengthen the educational experience
- **Enhanced focus on vocabulary building, test taking, and critical thinking skills** promotes academic achievement
- **New strategies and activities for the TOEFL® iBT** build invaluable test taking skills
- **New "Best Practices" approach** promotes excellence in language teaching

NEW to Interactions 1 Listening/Speaking:

- **All new content:** Chapter 10 Sports
- **Transparent chapter structure**—with consistent part headings, activity labeling, and clear guidance—strengthens the academic experience.
- **New "Student Book with Audio Highlights"** editions allow students to personalize the learning process by listening to dialogs and pronunciation activities multiple times
- **All-new *Interactions* photo program** features a cast of engaging, multi-ethnic students participating in North American college life
- **New vocabulary index** offers students and instructors a chapter-by-chapter list of target words
- **Online Learning Center features MP3 files** from the Student Book audio program for students to download onto portable digital audio players

---

* TOEFL is a registered trademark of Education Testing Service (ETS). This publication is not endorsed or approved by ETS.

Interactions/Mosaic
Best Practices

Our Interactions/Mosaic Silver Edition team has produced an edition that focuses on Best Practices, principles that contribute to excellent language teaching and learning. Our team of writers, editors, and teacher consultants has identified the following six interconnected Best Practices:

Making Use of Academic Content

Materials and tasks based on academic content and experiences give learning real purpose. Students explore real world issues, discuss academic topics, and study content-based and thematic materials.

Organizing Information

Students learn to organize thoughts and notes through a variety of graphic organizers that accommodate diverse learning and thinking styles.

Scaffolding Instruction

A scaffold is a physical structure that facilitates construction of a building. Similarly, scaffolding instruction is a tool used to facilitate language learning in the form of predictable and flexible tasks. Some examples include oral or written modeling by the teacher or students, placing information in a larger framework, and reinterpretation.

Activating Prior Knowledge

Students can better understand new spoken or written material when they connect to the content. Activating prior knowledge allows students to tap into what they already know, building on this knowledge, and stirring a curiosity for more knowledge.

Interacting with Others

Activities that promote human interaction in pair work, small group work, and whole class activities present opportunities for real world contact and real world use of language.

Cultivating Critical Thinking

Strategies for critical thinking are taught explicitly. Students learn tools that promote critical thinking skills crucial to success in the academic world.

Highlights of Interactions 1 Listening/Speaking Silver Edition

Full-color design showcases compelling instructional photos to strengthen the educational experience.

Interacting with Others
Questions and topical quotes stimulate interest, activate prior knowledge, and launch the topic of the unit.

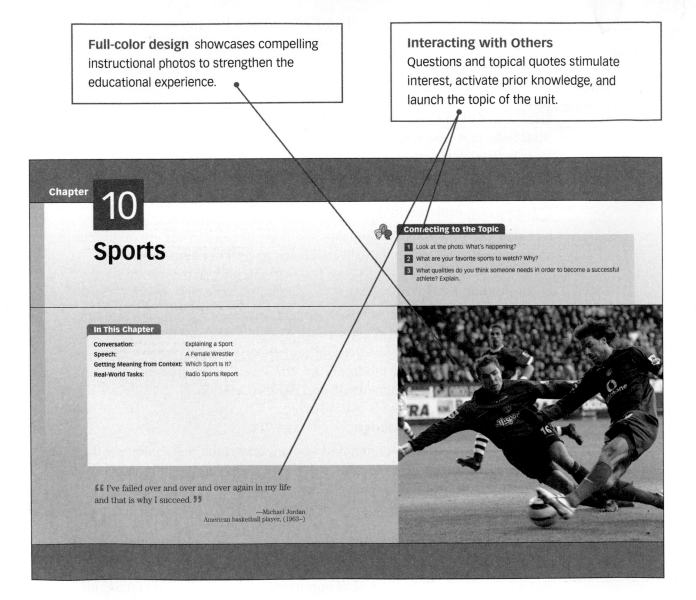

Chapter
10

Sports

Connecting to the Topic

1 Look at the photo. What's happening?

2 What are your favorite sports to watch? Why?

3 What qualities do you think someone needs in order to become a successful athlete? Explain.

In This Chapter

Conversation:	Explaining a Sport
Speech:	A Female Wrestler
Getting Meaning from Context:	Which Sport Is It?
Real-World Tasks:	Radio Sports Report

❝ I've failed over and over and over again in my life and that is why I succeed. ❞

—Michael Jordan
American basketball player, (1963–)

Making Use of Academic Content
Lectures, academic discussions, and conversations among university students explore stimulating topics.

Scaffolding Instruction
Instruction and practice build gradually to support student in the listening tasks.

Listen

3 Listening for Main Ideas Listen to advice from a radio show called, "Eating Right!" As you listen, answer this question:

What are some important things you can do to eat right?

4 Taking Notes on Specific Information Listen again. This time, complete the chart with Bob and Pam's advice. Try to catch as many details as you can.

Things You Should Eat	Reasons	Examples
vegetables	fiber.	carrots.

Things You Shouldn't Eat or Drink	Reasons	Examples

After You Listen

5 Summarizing Ideas

1. Compare notes with a partner. Together, summarize in complete sentences the advice you heard. Include reasons and examples. Tell your partner if you have tried any of these ideas for healthy eating.

Example

You should eat a carrot for a snack because it's a vegetable that has . . .

2. With your class, make a list on the board of additional dos and don'ts about healthy eating. Tell the class which ones you have tried and if they worked well.

6 Using Vocabulary Discuss the following questions with a partner. Use the underlined vocabulary in your answers.

1. Which meal are you least likely to skip, and which meal are you most likely to skip? Why?

2. Bodybuilders, football players, and other athletes often try to gain weight and strength. What specific types of food would you suggest for these people to eat?

3. What do you eat or drink that you know may be bad for your teeth? Would you consider stopping? Would you cut down on these things? How do you try to avoid tooth decay?

4. Do you ever think about the number of calories in certain foods you eat? Do you read food labels? Why, or why not?

5. Which of your favorite foods do you think are the best sources of vitamins and minerals?

6. What kinds of foods do you eat to get fiber in your diet?

Talk It Over

7 Comparing Eating Habits "Eating habits" are your eating customs. They include when, where, and what you eat. Take notes in the chart below. Then use the chart to talk about differences between your eating habits at home and the way you eat when you travel somewhere.

	When I'm at Home	When I Travel
1. what you eat for breakfast, lunch, and dinner	I eat rice for breakfast.	I eat cereal for breakfast.
2. the time and size of meals and snacks		
3. the price of food		
4. restaurants		
5. table manners		

Cultivating Critical Thinking
Critical thinking strategies and activities equip students with the skills they need for academic achievement.

Highlights of Interactions 1
Listening/Speaking Silver Edition

Activating Prior Knowledge
Pre-listening activities place the listening in context and allow the student to listen actively.

Enhanced focus on vocabulary building promotes academic achievement.

Part 1 Conversation: Learning New Customs

Before You Listen

1 Prelistening Questions Before you listen, talk about travel with a partner.

▲ Salma talking on her cell phone.

1. Discuss the situation in the photo. Why shouldn't Salma use her cell phone?

2. Do you know the expression "When in Rome, do as the Romans do"? Tell about a time when you followed this advice.

3. How do you feel when you travel to a new place, meet new people, and experience new customs? Circle the words in the box that describe how you feel. Explain or give examples of times that you have had these feelings.

excited	careful	afraid	shy	nervous
energetic	homesick	worried	interested	curious

2 Previewing Vocabulary Listen to the underlined words. You will hear these words in the conversation. Then use the context to guess their meanings. Write your guesses in the spaces.

Contexts	Meanings
1. My first impression of my new boss was not good. He seemed strict and unfriendly when I first met him, but now I like him.	
2. I don't like getting up at 6 A.M., but I am used to it now because I've been doing it every day for three years.	
3. Mr. and Mrs. Haley like to travel to exotic places. They like unusual and interesting vacations.	
4. If you don't finish your food in an American restaurant, you can take the remaining food home in a doggie bag.	
5. When I arrived in the U.S., I was amazed by the number of large cars on the road. There were so many! We have only small cars where I'm from.	
6. Our teacher has not given us a lot of homework so far, but maybe she'll give us more next week.	
7. When we finished dinner, we saved the leftovers in the refrigerator.	

Listen

3 Listening for Main Ideas Kenji is having lunch with Yolanda and her friend Salma, who is visiting from Lebanon. Close your book as you listen to the conversation. Listen for the answers to these questions.

1. What is Salma's impression of the United States?

2. What surprised Salma in the restaurant?

3. What is Kenji's advice about customs in the United States?

Compare and discuss answers with a partner.

Organizing Information
Graphic organizers provide tools for organizing information and ideas.

New strategies and activities for the TOEFL® iBT build invaluable test taking skills.

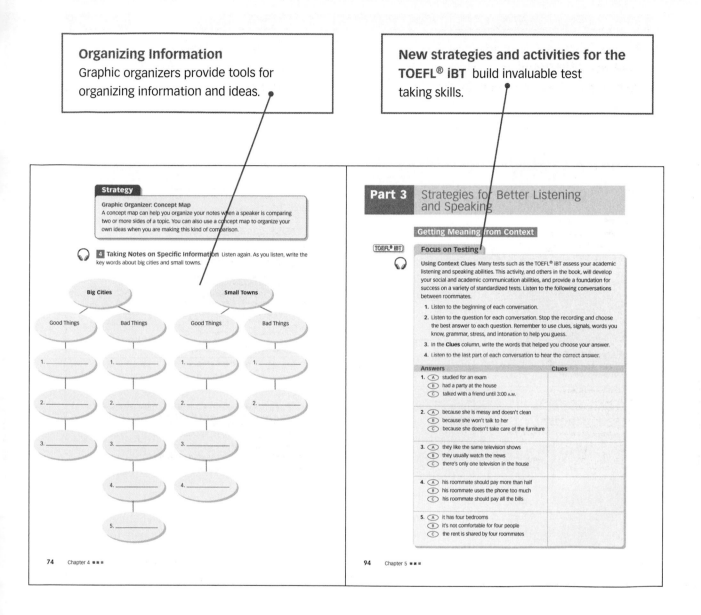

Strategy

Graphic Organizer: Concept Map
A concept map can help you organize your notes when a speaker is comparing two or more sides of a topic. You can also use a concept map to organize your own ideas when you are making this kind of comparison.

4 Taking Notes on Specific Information Listen again. As you listen, write the key words about big cities and small towns.

Big Cities

Good Things   Bad Things

1. _____   1. _____
2. _____   2. _____
3. _____   3. _____
        4. _____
        5. _____

Small Towns

Good Things   Bad Things

1. _____   1. _____
2. _____   2. _____
3. _____
4. _____

Part 3   Strategies for Better Listening and Speaking

Getting Meaning from Context

TOEFL® iBT   **Focus on Testing**

Using Context Clues Many tests such as the TOEFL® iBT assess your academic listening and speaking abilities. This activity, and others in the book, will develop your social and academic communication abilities, and provide a foundation for success on a variety of standardized tests. Listen to the following conversations between roommates.

1. Listen to the beginning of each conversation.
2. Listen to the question for each conversation. Stop the recording and choose the best answer to each question. Remember to use clues, signals, words you know, grammar, stress, and intonation to help you guess.
3. In the **Clues** column, write the words that helped you choose your answer.
4. Listen to the last part of each conversation to hear the correct answer.

Answers	Clues
1. (A) studied for an exam (B) had a party at the house (C) talked with a friend until 3:00 A.M.	
2. (A) because she is messy and doesn't clean (B) because she won't talk to her (C) because she doesn't take care of the furniture	
3. (A) they like the same television shows (B) they usually watch the news (C) there's only one television in the house	
4. (A) his roommate should pay more than half (B) his roommate uses the phone too much (C) his roommate should pay all the bills	
5. (A) it has four bedrooms (B) it's not comfortable for four people (C) the rent is shared by four roommates	

Scope and Sequence

Chapter	Listening	Speaking	Critical Thinking
1 Academic Life Around the World page 2	■ Listening for main ideas ■ Listening for details ■ Listening to an advisor's presentation ■ Distinguishing among -s endings	■ Introducing yourself and others ■ Leaving telephone messages ■ Giving telephone messages ■ Discussing body language	■ Guessing meaning from context ■ Interpreting a photo ■ Predicting the content before listening ■ Distinguishing main ideas from details ■ Summarizing ideas using key words
2 Experiencing Nature page 22	■ Listening for main ideas ■ Listening for details ■ Distinguishing between *can* and *can't* ■ Listening to a story about camping ■ Listening to weather forecasts	■ Discussing vacation plans ■ Talking about abilities ■ Talking about the weather and seasons ■ Expressing likes and dislikes	■ Interpreting a photo ■ Using a T-chart to compare two sides of a topic ■ Distinguishing main ideas from details ■ Summarizing ideas using key words
3 Living to Eat, or Eating to Live? page 40	■ Listening for main ideas ■ Listening for details ■ Distinguishing between *teens* and *tens* ■ Listening to radio advice on healthy eating ■ Connecting native foods to their locations	■ Interviewing people about food shopping ■ Using count and non-count nouns in questions ■ Comparing eating habits at home and when traveling ■ Ordering food ■ Refusing food politely	■ Interpreting a photo ■ Interviewing with possible follow-up questions ■ Taking notes on causes and effects ■ Explaining a process ■ Speculating on the outcome of a situation

Vocabulary Building	Pronunciation	Focus on Testing
■ Expressions used in introductions ■ Terms related to arrival and orientation at college or university ■ Casual expressions for making friends ■ Instructions (imperatives) used in telephone messages	■ Identifying and practicing stressed words ■ Comparing reduced and unreduced pronunciation ■ Pronouncing -s endings	■ Using context clues to guess the correct answers to questions **TOEFL® IBT**
■ Terms to express abilities ■ Terms to describe the weather and seasons ■ Terms to talk about likes and dislikes	■ Identifying and practicing stressed words ■ Comparing reduced and unreduced pronunciation ■ Pronouncing *can* and *can't*	■ Using context clues to identify seasons **TOEFL® IBT**
■ Terms used in shopping for food at a market ■ Terms to talk about healthy eating ■ Count and non-count nouns to express quantities of food ■ Terms for ordering food in a restaurant ■ Polite refusals	■ Identifying and practicing stressed words ■ Comparing reduced and unreduced pronunciation ■ Pronouncing *teens* and *tens*	■ Using context clues to guess locations **TOEFL® IBT**

Vocabulary Building	Pronunciation	Focus on Testing
■ Terms to describe locations in a city ■ Expressions for giving and asking for directions	■ Identifying and practicing stressed words ■ Comparing reduced and unreduced pronunciation	■ Using context clues to guess locations TOEFL® iBT
■ Terms to talk about apartments ■ Common verbs related to moving ■ Expressions for making and answering requests ■ Verbs and frequency expressions to explain homecare	■ Identifying and practicing stressed words ■ Comparing reduced and unreduced pronunciation ■ Pronouncing past tense -ed endings	■ Using context clues to guess what speakers are implying TOEFL® iBT
■ Adjectives describing feelings ■ Expressions for apologizing ■ Correct use of 'I'm sorry' vs. 'Excuse me' ■ Terms used related to table settings and table manners	■ Identifying and practicing stressed words ■ Comparing reduced and unreduced pronunciation	■ Using context clues to identify culturally incorrect behaviors TOEFL® iBT
■ Terms connected with a health club ■ Terms describing symptoms and remedies ■ Expressions for giving and accepting advice ■ Terms used in expressing agreement or disagreement	■ Identifying and practicing stressed words ■ Contrasting rising and falling intonation in tag questions	■ Using context clues to identify unusual details within situations TOEFL® iBT

Vocabulary Building	Pronunciation	Focus on Testing
■ Terms for expressing opinions, agreeing and disagreeing ■ Terms related to TV-watching habits ■ Terms to describe types of TV programs	■ Identifying and practicing stressed words ■ Comparing reduced and unreduced pronunciation	■ Using context clues to identify products and services in commercials TOEFL® iBT
■ Terms connected with friendship and dating ■ Exclamations ■ Expressions used in giving and accepting compliments ■ Terms to talk about personal qualities and compatibility ■ Terms connected with parties and common entertainment activities	■ Identifying and practicing stressed words ■ Using appropriate intonation with exclamations	■ Using context clues to guess the nature of interpersonal relationships TOEFL® iBT
■ Nouns vs. verbs to describe sports and athletes ■ Terms used in a sportscast ■ Terms for giving instructions ■ Terms to ensure comprehension ■ Terms to ask for clarification	■ Identifying and practicing stressed words ■ Comparing reduced and unreduced pronunciation ■ Pronouncing the North American *t* ■ Dropping the *h* sound in unstressed words	■ Using context clues to identify different sports TOEFL® iBT

Name: Ming
Nationality: Chinese

Name: Peter
Nationality: Puerto Rican

Name: Jack
Nationality: American

Name: Kenji
Nationality: Japanese

Name: Ali
Nationality: American

Name: Salma
Nationality: Lebanese

Name: Yolanda
Nationality: American

Name: Nancy
Nationality: American

Name: Andrew
Nationality: American

Name: Lee
Nationality: Korean

Academic Life Around the World

❝ Teachers open the door. You enter by yourself. **❞**

—Chinese proverb

Connecting to the Topic

1 Look at the people in the photo. Where are they? What's their relationship to one another?

2 Think of some of your close friends. How did you meet them?

3 What types of information are important to get on the first day of a new class?

Before You Listen

 1 Prelistening Questions Answer the questions with a partner.

▲ Jack, Peter, and Ming in the lobby of their building

1. What do you say when you meet someone for the first time?

2. What body language or gestures do you use when you meet someone new? For example, do you hug or shake hands?

3. What body language or gestures do you use when you greet a good friend? A classmate? A co-worker?

2 Previewing Vocabulary Listen to these words and phrases from the conversation. Then complete the sentences with the words and phrases.

Verbs
came over (come over)
move into
sound
stop by
take

Expressions
call me
No kidding!
you guys*

1. His name is Kenji. I don't think that's an English name. It _____*sounds*_____ Japanese.

2. We have a new house, but we can't _____ it until next month.

3. My friend is in the hospital. I will _____ tomorrow and bring her flowers.

4. You have seven brothers and one sister? _____

5. My name is Robert Browning. But please, _____ Bob.

6. I was born in the United States, but my parents _____ from Korea 35 years ago.

7. If your major is Asian Studies, I'm sure you have to _____ Chinese and probably some other Asian languages, too.

8. Bye, Tom. Bye, Reka. See _____ tomorrow.

Listen

 3 Listening for Main Ideas Jack, Peter, and Ming are students at Faber College. They meet in the lobby of their apartment building. Close your book as you listen. Prepare to answer these questions:

1. Which students already know each other?

2. What information do you find out about Ming?

3. What will the students do after this conversation?

Compare and discuss your answers with a partner.

 4 Listening for Details Listen again if necessary. Write *T* if a statement is true and *F* if it is false.

_____ **1.** Ming was born in Hong Kong.

_____ **2.** Peter plans to take a Chinese class.

_____ **3.** Jack and Peter are roommates.

_____

* "You guys" is a very informal expression used only with people you know very well.

Stress

In spoken English, important words are stressed. This means that they are spoken louder, longer, or higher than other words. Stressed words usually give the most important information. These kinds of words are usually stressed: verbs, nouns, adjectives, adverbs, numbers, and negatives like "isn't," "don't," and "can't."

Example

My **name** is **Peter.**

I'm in **apartment two-twelve.**

Maybe you could **help** me.

We're on the **same floor.**

5 Listening for Stressed Words Listen to the conversation again. Some of the stressed words are missing. During each pause, repeat the phrase or sentence. Then fill in the blanks with the words you hear.

Jack: _____! How are you _____?

Peter: Hi. You're . . . _____, right?

Jack: Yeah. And, _____, you're . . . ?

Peter: Peter. Peter Riley.

Jack: Oh, yeah, we _____ on _____ last week. Peter, this is my _____, Ming Lee. She's just _____ into the _____.

Peter: Hi, Ming Lee.

Ming: _____ to _____ you. You can just _____ me Ming. Lee's my _____.

Peter: Oh. Ming. That _____ . . .

Ming: Chinese.

Peter: Oh. So, you're from . . .

Ming: . . . from San Francisco. My parents _____ _____ from Hong Kong before I was _____.

Peter: Oh, that's cool. Actually, uh, I was _____ of taking _____ this _____. Maybe you could _____ me.

Ming: Well, my Chinese really isn't very _____ . . .

Jack: Uh, listen, Peter. We're _____ _____. Do

you want to get _____ to _____ with us?

Peter: Sorry, I _____. I have to go _____ my

new _____.

Jack: Oh, OK. Well, _____ by sometime. I'm up in

_____.

Peter: Hey, I'm on the same _____. I'm in _____.

Jack: No kidding . . .

Peter: Well, _____ _____ you, Ming. I'm sure

I'll _____ you guys _____.

Ming and Jack: See you later.

Now read the conversation with two other classmates. Practice stressing words correctly.

Reductions

In spoken English, important words are usually stressed. Other words are not stressed; they are often *reduced* or *shortened.* These kinds of words are often reduced: prepositions, articles, pronouns, forms of the verb *to be,* and the words *and, or,* and *but.*

Unreduced Pronunciation	**Reduced Pronunciation***
Do you want to . . .	D'ya wanna . . .
How are you doing?	How're ya doing?
Nice to meet you.	Niceta meetcha.

Speakers usually use unreduced pronunciation in formal speech and reduced pronunciation in informal speech.

6 Comparing Unreduced and Reduced Pronunciation The following sentences come from the conversation. Listen for the difference between unreduced and reduced pronunciation. Repeat both forms after the speaker.

Unreduced Pronunciation	**Reduced Pronunciation***
1. Hi! How are you doing?	Hi! How're ya doing?
2. Do you want to get something to eat with us?	D'ya wanna get something to eat with us?
3. I have to meet my new roommate.	I hafta meet my new roommate.
4. I'll see you guys soon.	I'll see ya guys soon.

* Note: The reduced forms are not acceptable spellings in written English.

7 Listening for Reductions Listen to the following sentences. You'll hear the reduced pronunciations of some words. Repeat each sentence during the pause. Then write the unreduced forms of the missing words in the blanks.

1. _____ _____ _____ feeling?

2. _____ _____ in an hour.

3. Jack, _____ _____ _____ _____ eat at the cafeteria?

4. When _____ _____ _____ _____ meet your roommate?

With a partner, read the sentences. Practice reduced pronunciation.

After You Listen

8 Reviewing Vocabulary Work in pairs: Student A should look at page 200. Student B should look at page 204.

Pronunciation

THE -S ENDING

The -s at the end of verbs, plural nouns, and possessive nouns can be pronounced differently, depending on the end of the word.

/iz/ after -ch, -sh, -s, -x, and -z endings.

Examples
teaches, boxes, buses, brushes

/s/ after voiceless -k, -f, -p, or -t endings.

Examples
drinks, stops, hits, puts

/z/ after voiced endings.

Examples
carries, brings, father's, rides

9 Distinguishing Among -s Endings Listen and write the words. Then check the sound you hear. The first one is done as an example.

		/iz/	/s/	/z/
1.	_plays_	☐	☐	☑
2.	_____	☐	☐	☐
3.	_____	☐	☐	☐
4.	_____	☐	☐	☐
5.	_____	☐	☐	☐
6.	_____	☐	☐	☐
7.	_____	☐	☐	☐
8.	_____	☐	☐	☐
9.	_____	☐	☐	☐
10.	_____	☐	☐	☐

10 Pronouncing -s Endings Work with a partner. Ask each other the following questions and answer them in complete sentences. Pay attention to the pronunciation of the -s endings.

1. Where does your teacher work?

2. What does he or she teach?

3. How much homework does your teacher give you?

4. When does your class begin?

5. When does your class end?

6. How many books does a college student usually buy each term?

7. How long does it take for you to get to school?

8. What kind of things do you bring to school every day?

9. How many subjects did you study in high school?

10. What does a student do if he or she wants to ask a question in class?

▲ How much homework does your teacher give you?

Using Language Functions

INTRODUCING YOURSELF AND OTHERS

Read this part of the conversation between Peter, Jack, and Ming. Notice the words Jack uses to introduce Ming.

Jack: Peter, this is my friend, Ming Lee.
Peter: Hi, Ming.
Ming: Nice to meet you.

The following expressions are often used when English speakers introduce themselves or others.

Functions	Expressions		
	Speaker A	**Speaker B**	**Speaker C**
Introducing Others	Sharon, this is my friend, Kim.	Hi, Kim.	Nice to meet you.
	Linda, I'd like you to meet my roommate, Evan.	Good to meet you, Evan.	You, too.
	Mom, I'd like to introduce you to my teacher, Mr. Saunders.	Pleasure to meet you.	Same here.
Introducing Yourself	Hi, I'm Judy. I'm your neighbor in 206.	Nice to meet you.	
	My name is Denise.	Hi, Denise. I'm Ricardo.	

11 **Making Introductions** Practice introducing classmates to each other.

1. Sit in a circle if possible.

2. Write your first name on a card and put the card on your desk for everyone to see.

3. Ask a student next to you three or four questions like these:
   - Where are you from?
   - What do you do?
   - Do you work?
   - Do you have a hobby?

4. Now introduce your partner to several other students in the class.

   Example Jose, this is Noriko. Noriko, this is Jose. Jose is from Mexico. He's a full-time student. He enjoys sports and reading.

5. Put away your name cards. Walk around the room and see how many names you can remember. If you can't remember someone's name, use expressions like these:

- Excuse me, what was your name again?
- I'm sorry, can you tell me your name again?
- I'm sorry, I didn't catch your name.
- You're Paula, right?

 12 Role-Play: A First Meeting Joe and Meena are students at the same college. They meet for the first time at the student cafeteria when their trays collide. What do they say? How do they feel? Will they meet again? Prepare a conversation with a partner. Memorize your lines and put on a skit for the class.

Before You Listen

1 Prelistening Questions You will hear a short speech by a school advisor on the first day of an English language program. Before you listen, answer these questions with a partner.

1. What usually happens on the first day in a language program?

2. What information do students probably get?

3. How did you feel on the first day of your English program or course?

2 Previewing Vocabulary Listen to the underlined words and phrases. You will hear the underlined words and phrases in the presentation. Write the letter of the correct definition beside each sentence.

Sentences

1. _____ My advisor always gives me good advice about what classes to take.

2. _____ David has a busy schedule. He has two classes in the morning and three classes in the afternoon.

3. _____ Many large universities in North America have swimming pools, tennis courts, and other sports facilities.

4. _____ New workers in my company go to an orientation on their first day of work to learn all the necessary information about the company rules.

5. _____ I'm not sure if my English is intermediate or advanced, so I have to take a placement test.

Definitions

a. A list of activities and their times

b. Places or areas for special activities

c. An exam to find a student's correct place or level

d. A person who helps you plan your courses

e. An informational meeting

Strategy

Hints for Taking Notes

- Don't try to write everything you hear.
- Focus only on important information.
- Don't write complete sentences; write key words only.
- Don't write small details.

3 Listening for Main Ideas

▲ An advisor gives a presentation to new students

1. Listen to the advisor's presentation. To help you remember the main ideas, take notes on a piece of paper. (Complete this before continuing to item 2.)

2. Look at the notes below. They show the main ideas of the presentation. Do your notes have the same points? If yes, then you understood the main ideas!

Main Ideas

Speaker: Gina Richards
Schedule Today:
- *Placement Test*
- *Orientation*
- *Campus Tour*

4 **Listening for Specific Information** Listen again. This time, add details to the main ideas.

Main Ideas and Details

Speaker: Gina Richards
Schedule Today:

- Placement Test

_____

- Orientation

_____

- Campus Tour

_____

After You Listen

 5 **Summarizing Ideas** Compare your notes with a partner's. Summarize the presentation in your own words. As you speak, look at your notes to help you remember.

Example In this speech, Gina Richards speaks to new students in an English program. Gina is an advisor. She tells them about . . .

 6 **Reviewing Vocabulary** Ask and answer the following questions with a partner. Use the underlined vocabulary in your answers.

1. What is your daily <u>schedule</u> on Mondays? Tell the times and activities.

2. Talk about the <u>placement test</u> you took in your language school. How long was it? How many parts did it have? Which part was the most difficult? If your school doesn't have a placement test, who decided your English level?

3. Discuss what type of information you might hear:
   at an <u>orientation</u> for first-year students at a college or university.
   at an orientation for a group of tourists visiting your hometown or city.
   at an orientation for parents before the first day of kindergarten.

4. What kinds of <u>facilities</u> does your school have? Are they free or do you have to pay to use them? What new facilities would you like your school to add?

5. What is necessary to be a good <u>advisor</u>? At your school, who is a good advisor to you? How does she or he help you?

Part 3 | Strategies for Better Listening and Speaking

Focus on Testing

Getting Meaning from Context

If you don't understand everything that English speakers say, use your guessing ability. How?

- Listen to clues, or signals, that help you guess.
- Words that you already know can be clues to new words.
- Grammar, stress, and intonation can also be clues to meaning.

Read the sentence below. Can you guess the meaning of the new word from all the other words you know?

Basic English is a prerequisite before you can take Intermediate English.

clue   new word   clue   clue

You can guess that *prerequisite* means *something that is necessary before something else.*

Many tests such as the TOEFL® iBT measure your academic listening and speaking abilities. This activity, and others in the book, will develop your social and academic communication abilities, and provide a foundation for success on a variety of standardized tests.

Using Context Clues Listen to a conversation between Ming, Peter, and Peter's new roommate, Kenji.

1. The conversation is in five parts. Listen to the beginning of each part. Then listen to the question.

2. Stop the recording after the question and choose the best answer to each question.

3. In the Clues column, write the words that helped you choose your answer.

4. Start the recording again. Listen to the last part of each conversation to hear the correct answer.

---

* TOEFL is a registered trademark of Education Testing Service (ETS). This publication is not endorsed or approved by ETS.

Answers	Clues
1. (A) in class (B) at the student orientation (C) at a pizza restaurant	*cheese, pepperoni, mushrooms, hungry, medium, large*
2. (A) testing advisor (B) chemistry professor (C) teaching assistant	
3. (A) It's different from Japan. (B) It's a terrible place. (C) It's similar to Japan.	
4. (A) go to the tennis courts between 8 A.M. and 5 P.M. (B) telephone between 8 A.M. and 5 P.M. (C) pay between $5 and $8	
5. (A) reserve a tennis court (B) play tennis together (C) go to class together	

Talk It Over

UNDERSTANDING BODY LANGUAGE

In face-to-face situations, body language—gestures, facial expressions, and eye contact—can give you important clues to help you understand the speaker.

 1 **Using Body Language** Now discuss what the gestures on the next page mean in different cultures.

Use body language to show the following situations.

1. You don't know the answer to the question.

2. You think that the class is boring.

3. You can't hear what someone is saying.

4. Someone on the phone is talking too much.

1 **Listening to Telephone Messages** When Peter and Kenji cannot answer their phone, people leave messages on their voice mail. Listen to each message. Write the important information in the spaces below. Then, compare your notes with a partner.

Example

WHILE YOU WERE OUT

To: _Kenji_

From: _Dr. Brown's office_

Message: _Can you change your appointment to Wednesday at 2:00? Dr. Brown can't see you on Tuesday._

Phone Number: _555-0162_

1.

WHILE YOU WERE OUT

To: _____

From: _____

Message: _____

_____

_____

_____

Phone Number: _____

2.

WHILE YOU WERE OUT

To: _____

From: _____

Message: _____

_____

_____

_____

Phone Number: _____

3.

WHILE YOU WERE OUT

To: _____

From: _____

Message: _____

_____

_____

_____

Phone Number: _____

4.

WHILE YOU WERE OUT

To: _____

From: _____

Message: _____

_____

_____

_____

Phone Number: _____

5.

WHILE YOU WERE OUT

To: _____

From: _____

Message: _____

_____

_____

_____

Phone Number: _____

6.

WHILE YOU WERE OUT

To: _____

From: _____

Message: _____

_____

_____

_____

Phone Number: _____

2 Role-Play: Giving Telephone Messages Work with a partner. Pretend you are Peter and Kenji. Look at your notes on pages 18 and 19. Take turns giving each other the messages.

Example

Kenji: Did I get any messages?

Peter: Yeah, Dr. Brown's office called.

Kenji: Oh, really? What did they say?

Peter: They want to change your appointment from Tuesday to Wednesday.

Kenji: Did they leave a phone number?

Peter: Uh-huh. It's 555-0162.

Telephone Numbers

When saying telephone numbers, English speakers will understand you better if you:

- pause after the area code.
- pause after the first three numbers, and between the next two pairs of numbers.
- raise your voice before every pause.
- lower your voice at the end.

Example

area code (310) 555-0162:

three-one-zero ∧ five-five-five ∧ zero-one ∧ six-two

3 Calling for Information Ming calls the college about a parking permit and talks to an administrative assistant. Listen to her conversation and complete the application form.

PARKING PERMIT APPLICATION

📖 FABER COLLEGE

Name: _____
          Last   *First*   *Middle initial*

Address: _____

Phone: _____

Car: _____
       Make   *Model*   *Year*

License plate: _____

☐ Fall Semester   ☐ Request handicap
                     parking space

☐ Spring Semester

☐ All year   Amount enclosed $ _____

---

4 Role-Play Compare your application form with a partner. Then role-play Ming and the administrative assistant discussing parking permits. Pronounce numbers carefully!

Self-Assessment Log

Check the words you learned in this chapter.

Nouns
- ❏ advisor
- ❏ facilities
- ❏ orientation
- ❏ placement test
- ❏ schedule

Verbs
- ❏ came over (come over)
- ❏ move into
- ❏ sound
- ❏ stop by
- ❏ take

Expressions
- ❏ call me
- ❏ No kidding!
- ❏ you guys

Check the things you did in this chapter. How well can you do each one?

	Very well	Fairly well	Not very well
I can listen to and practice stress and reductions.	❏	❏	❏
I can listen to and pronounce -s endings.	❏	❏	❏
I can introduce myself and others.	❏	❏	❏
I can take notes on a presentation.	❏	❏	❏
I can summarize my notes.	❏	❏	❏
I can guess meanings from context.	❏	❏	❏
I can understand and talk about body language.	❏	❏	❏
I can listen to and give telephone messages.	❏	❏	❏

Write about what you did in this chapter.

In this chapter,

I learned _____

_____

I liked _____

_____

Experiencing Nature

In This Chapter

Conversation:	Vacation Plans
Story:	Camping
Getting Meaning from Context:	Talking About Seasons
Real-World Tasks:	Listening to a Weather Forecast

❝ In every walk with nature, one receives far more than he seeks. ❞

—John Muir
American naturalist (1838–1914)

Connecting to the Topic

1 Look at the photo. What do you see? Would you like to be in this place? Why or why not?

2 What kinds of outdoor activities do you enjoy?

3 What is your favorite kind of weather? Why?

Before You Listen

 1 Prelistening Questions Look at the photo. Answer the questions with a partner.

▲ Jack, Ming, and Peter

1. What are Jack, Ming, and Peter thinking about?

2. Describe your perfect outdoor vacation. Where would you go? What would you do there?

2 Previewing Vocabulary Listen to these words and phrases from the conversation. Complete the sentences with these words and phrases.

Nouns	Verb	Adjectives	Expressions
chance of	get a tan	extra	how come
degrees		freezing	it's raining cats and dogs
weather forecast		sick of (verb + *-ing*)	

1. **A:** Wow. _____ you're all wet?

   B: Because _____ outside, and
   I forgot my umbrella.

2. In the summer, I love to lie in the sun and _____.

3. The weather report in the newspaper says there's a 90 percent

   _____ snow tomorrow. Be sure to dress warm.

4. It's 20 _____ Celsius* outside. You don't need a sweater.

5. When are we going to get to Las Vegas?
   We've been on the road for six hours.

   I am _____ driving.

6. **A:** Did you hear the

   _____

   for tomorrow on the news?

   B: Yes. It's going to be sunny and warm.
   A perfect day for the beach!

7. **A:** Why don't you turn on the heater?

   It's _____ in this

   room!

   B: It's broken. We'll have to sleep in
   our coats tonight.

8. Do you have an _____
   jacket? I forgot mine at home.

▲ It's raining cats and dogs.

Listen

3 Listening for Main Ideas Jack, Peter, and Ming are talking about weather and vacations. Close your book as you listen. Prepare to answer these questions.

1. Why does Peter want to go on vacation soon?

2. Where does Ming prefer to go on vacation?

3. What do Jack and Peter agree about?

Compare and discuss your answers with a partner.

_____

*Equal to about 68° Fahrenheit.

4 **Listening for Details** Listen again if necessary. Write *T* if a statement is true and *F* if it is false.

_____ **1.** It is almost the end of the school year.

_____ **2.** Jack has never tried skiing.

_____ **3.** The weather isn't going to be better tomorrow.

Stress

 5 **Listening for Stressed Words** Listen to the conversation again. Some of the stressed words are missing. During each pause, repeat the phrase or sentence. Then fill in the blanks with words you hear.

Peter: Wow. Look. It's raining cats and dogs—_____! I _____ this weather. When does winter _____ start?

Jack: Winter break? It's only _____.

Peter: I know, but I'm _____ of studying. I want to go someplace _____ and lie on the _____ for a week. Someplace where it's _____ and dry. Florida or Hawaii, maybe?

Jack: Yeah. Where we can go _____ and snorkeling and get a great _____. Now _____ my idea of a perfect vacation.

Ming: Not mine. I can't swim very well, and I _____ like lying in the _____.

Peter: Oh, yeah? How come?

Ming: I don't know. I just prefer the _____, especially in winter. I _____ snowboarding. In fact, I'm _____ to go to Bear Mountain with some friends in _____. Do you guys want to _____?

Jack: No thanks. I went there _____ year. I was _____ the whole time. Anyway, I don't know how to _____ very well. Last year I _____ about a hundred times.

Ming: Peter, how about you?

Peter: Sorry, I'm like Jack. I don't want to go _____ where it's

below 70 _____.

Jack: By the way, what's the _____ forecast for tomorrow?

Ming: The _____ as today. _____, cold, and a

90 percent _____ of rain.

Jack: Oh, no! I _____ my umbrella at the _____.

Ming: You can _____ mine. I've got an _____ one.

Now read the conversation with two other classmates. Practice stressing words correctly.

Reductions

6 Comparing Unreduced and Reduced Pronunciation The following sentences come from the conversation. Listen for the difference between unreduced and reduced pronunciation. Repeat both forms after the speaker.

Unreduced Pronunciation	**Reduced Pronunciation***
1. It's raining cats and dogs.	It's raining cats 'n' dogs.
2. I want to go someplace warm.	I <u>wanna</u> go someplace warm.
3. We can swim.	We <u>kin</u> swim.
4. I'm going to go to Bear Mountain.	I'm <u>gonna</u> go <u>ta</u> Bear Mountain.
5. How about you?	How <u>bouchu</u>?
6. I don't want to go.	I <u>donwanna</u> go.

7 Listening for Reductions Listen to the following conversation. You'll hear the reduced pronunciations of some words. Repeat each sentence during the pause. Then write the unreduced forms of the missing words in the blanks.

Jack: Hi, Ming. Hi, Peter.

Ming and Peter: Hey, Jack.

Ming: What's happening?

Jack: I'm going to the campus recreation center. _____

_____ _____ _____ come?

Ming: What are you _____ _____ do there?

Jack: Well, it's a nice day. We _____ swim _____ lie in the sun.

---

* Note: The underlined forms are not acceptable spellings in written English.

Ming: Thanks, but I _____ _____ _____ go. I'm too tired.

Jack: How _____ _____, Peter?

Peter: I can't. I've _____ _____ stay at home _____ study. Maybe tomorrow.

With a partner, repeat the dialogue. Practice reduced pronunciation.

After You Listen

 8 Using Vocabulary Discuss the following questions with a partner. Use the underlined vocabulary in your answers.

1. When you are <u>sick of</u> studying, what do you do to relax?

2. In your hometown, what is the coldest temperature, and what is the hottest temperature? (Use the word <u>degrees</u> in your answer.)

3. What is a safe way to <u>get a tan</u>?

4. Are you afraid to drive if <u>it's raining cats and dogs</u>? How much <u>extra</u> time do you give yourself when you drive in bad weather?

5. What is the <u>chance of rain</u> tomorrow in the area where you live?

6. What's the best place to get the <u>weather forecast</u>: TV, newspaper, or Internet?

7. Which is worse for you: to be <u>freezing</u> or to be too hot?

Pronunciation

 CAN OR CAN'T

Notice the difference between the pronunciations of *can* and *can't* in the following sentences.

I *can* méet you tomorrow.   I *can't* méet you tomorrow.

Can is unstressed, so the vowel is reduced. It sounds like "kin." Stress only the main verb:

can méet.

Can't is stressed, so the vowel is not reduced. Stress both *can't* and the main verb:

can't méet.

9 Distinguishing Between *Can* and *Can't* Listen and repeat each statement. Circle *Can* if the statement is affirmative and *Can't* if the statement is negative.

1. Can	Can't	**6.** Can	Can't
2. Can	Can't	**7.** Can	Can't
3. Can	Can't	**8.** Can	Can't
4. Can	Can't	**9.** Can	Can't
5. Can	Can't	**10.** Can	Can't

Using Language Functions

TALKING ABOUT ABILITIES

You can use *can* and *can't* to talk about abilities.

> **Example** Ming can ski, but she can't swim.

Here are some other expressions for talking about what you can and can't do:

I'm (not) able to (+ verb)

I (don't) know how to (+ verb)

I wish I could (+ verb)

I'm (not) good at (+ verb + -*ing*)

I'm (not) really good at (+ verb + -*ing*)

Strategy

Graphic Organizer: T-Chart

T-charts can help you organize and compare two different sides of a topic.
For example:

- You can compare the advantages and disadvantages of an idea to help you make a decision.
- You can compare facts and opinions.
- You can list the strengths and weaknesses of an idea or of something you read or listen to.

Advantages/Disadvantages T-Chart

Topic: _____

Advantages	Disadvantages

10 Talking About Abilities Complete this chart. Then tell a partner about your abilities. Use *can, can't,* and the expressions from the list on page 29.

Abilities	
Things I Am Good At	Things I Am Not Good At
1.	1.
2.	2.
3.	3.
4.	4.

Part 2 Story: Camping

Before You Listen

1 Prelistening Questions You will hear a story about camping. Before you listen, answer these questions with a partner.

1. Have you ever gone camping? Tell about this experience. Where did you go? When? With whom?

2. Why do many people enjoy camping?

3. What unpleasant or dangerous things can happen while camping?

2 Previewing Vocabulary Listen to the underlined words and phrases. You will hear the underlined words and phrases in a story. Write the letter of the correct definition beside each sentence.

Sentences

1. _____ The view at the top of the mountain was incredible. The sunset was orange and purple.

2. _____ Please clean your muddy shoes before you come inside the house.

3. _____ When I'm sick of being in the city, I go hiking in the mountains.

4. _____ After the rain stopped, the sky was clear and sunny.

5. _____ After six months in another country, I couldn't wait to see my family again.

6. _____ Don't be scared of the dog; she is very sweet and gentle.

Definitions

a. afraid

b. walking out in nature

c. wanted to do something very much

d. unbelievable; very surprising

e. covered with wet earth

f. not cloudy

Listen

 3 Listening for Main Ideas A man and a woman are checking into a motel. They tell the manager a very unusual story. As you listen, answer these questions.

1. What starts all of the trouble?

2. What happens to the couple's clothes?

 **4 Taking Notes on Specific Information** Listen to the story again. Fill in the missing key information in the notes below. Remember:

- Don't try to write everything you hear. Write the important information only.

- Don't write complete sentences; write key words only.

▲ An unexpected visitor

1. decided to go _____

2. weather was _____

3. after 1/2 hr started to _____

4. hiked back to _____ to change _____

5. couldn't find _____

6. went back _____

7. saw _____ wearing _____

8. felt _____

9. problem now: _____

After You Listen

5 Summarizing Ideas

1. Compare your notes with a partner. Summarize the story in your own words. As you speak, look at your notes to help you remember.

2. In groups of three, play the roles of the man, the woman, and the hotel manager from the story. Don't read the script. Use your notes to help you remember the story.

6 Reviewing Vocabulary Talk about the picture below. Use the new vocabulary as you describe what is happening.

Noun	Adjectives	Expression
hiking	clear	I can't wait to . . .
	incredible	
	muddy	
	scared	

▲ Three hikers

Talk It Over

7 Fact or Fiction Game

1. Tell the class about a dangerous, unusual, or exciting experience that you had in nature. Your teacher will give you a card. If the card says "Fact," you must tell a true story. If the card says "Fiction," tell an imaginary story, but make it sound real.

2. After each story, the class will take a vote: how many people think the story was fact? How many think it was fiction? See which student in your class is the best storyteller—or the most creative!

8 **Role-Play** Discuss the following questions.

1. What does the sign in the photo mean? Why do you think camping areas and parks have signs like this?

2. Does your country have strong laws against littering (throwing paper and garbage on the ground or street)? Why do you think some countries have strong laws against littering? How does litter affect the environment?

▲ A common sign in U.S. parks

Look at the pictures and read the description of the situation. In groups of three (George, Lou, and Rick), role-play the situation. The following expressions may help you express your ideas:

Explaining Rules

You need to . . .   It's against the rules to . . .

You shouldn't . . .   You're not allowed to . . .

George and Lou are brothers. They have just spent a wonderful weekend camping. Now they're getting ready to leave, but they are leaving their campsite dirty and full of trash. Rick is a park ranger. He stops the brothers to explain their responsibilities and to ask them to clean up. Make up your own ending.

Getting Meaning from Context

1 **Prelistening Discussion** Before you listen, talk about seasons with a partner.

1. Identify the seasons in the photos (winter, spring, summer, or fall) and describe the weather in each one.

2. Do you know of any countries that don't have four seasons? Describe the weather in those countries.

Focus on Testing

Using Context Clues

Many tests such as the TOEFL® iBT measure your academic listening and speaking abilities. This activity, and others in the book, will develop your social and academic communication abilities, and provide a foundation for success on a variety of standardized tests. You are going to hear five conversations about seasons. As you listen to each conversation, write *winter, spring, summer,* or *fall* in the **Seasons** column. After each conversation, stop the recording and write the words that helped you choose the season. Compare your answers and clues with a partner.

Seasons	Clues
1.	
2.	
3.	
4.	
5.	

Talk It Over

2 **Talking About Seasons** Talk with a partner about seasons in New York. Work in pairs: Student A and Student B. Follow the instructions below.

1. Student A, look at page 200, and Student B, look at page 204.

2. Ask your partner questions about the missing information in your chart.

3. Write your partner's answers in the blank spaces on your chart. When you finish, your charts should match.

Examples

When is summer? Or, what are the summer months?
What's the weather like in the spring?

1 Listening for Temperatures

Listen to these conversations about the weather. Circle the temperatures you hear.

1. 19   95   99
2. 80s   18   8
3. 13   30   30s
4. 14   40   44
5. 103   130   133
6. 30s   30   13
7. –13   30   3
8. 70   70s   17

▲ A thermometer

Language Tip

Weather reports often say that the temperature is **"in the 30s"** (40s, 50s, etc.). **"In the 30s"** means that the temperature is anywhere between 30 and 39 degrees.

2 Talking About Temperatures

Your teacher will give each student the name of a city. Find today's temperatures around the world in a newspaper or on the Internet. Tell the class today's temperatures in the city your teacher gives you.

Example

Teacher: Sydney, Australia

Student: The high temperature will be 75 degrees Fahrenheit.
The low temperature will be 52.
Today's average temperatures will be in the 70s.

3 Previewing Vocabulary Listen to the underlined words and phrases. You will hear the underlined words in a weather forecast. Write the letter of the correct definition beside each sentence.

Sentences

1. _____ Take an umbrella. There's a chance of showers later.

2. _____ Take a sweater. It's chilly outside.

3. _____ The overnight temperature will be 20 degrees.

4. _____ The sky is partly cloudy. It's not a good day for the beach.

5. _____ The weather forecast says we can expect fair skies this weekend. Let's go fishing!

Definitions

a. clear, not rainy

b. short periods of rain

c. during the night

d. clear in some places and cloudy in others

e. a little cold

4 Listening to a Weather Forecast Ming is watching the weather forecast. Listen to the report and use the chart to take notes about the weekend weather.

▲ A TV reporter giving a weather forecast

	Friday	Saturday	Sunday	Monday
Sky: (Cloudy? Fair?)				
Temperature				
High:				
Low:				
Rain: (Yes? No?)				

Work in groups of four. Each student summarizes the information for one day.

Example

   Student 1: On Friday it will be partly cloudy with showers during the night.

   Student 2: On Saturday . . .

Using Language Functions

EXPRESSIONS FOR TALKING ABOUT ACTIVITIES YOU LIKE AND DISLIKE

Likes	Dislikes
I like/love (*to* + verb/verb + *-ing*).	I don't like/dislike/hate (*to* + verb/verb + *-ing*).
I enjoy (verb + *-ing*).	I'm not crazy about (noun).
It's OK/all right/fun/good /great/wonderful.	I don't care for (noun).
I'm crazy about (noun).	It's awful/terrible.
	I can't stand it.

 5 **Interview** Interview a partner about activities he or she likes or dislikes in each season. Complete the chart with your partner's answers.

Example

You ask: What do you like to do in the (summer)?

What's your favorite (winter) sport?

What activities do you dislike in (winter)?

Your partner answers: I like waterskiing in the summer.

My favorite winter "sport" is watching television!

I hate driving in the snow, but I enjoy making a snowman.

	Fall	Winter	Spring	Summer
Sports				
Other Activities (likes)				
Other Activities (dislikes)				

Self-Assessment Log

Check the words you learned in this chapter.

Nouns	**Verbs**	**Adjectives**	**Expressions**
❏ chance of	❏ get a tan	❏ chilly	❏ couldn't wait
❏ degrees		❏ clear	(can't wait)
❏ fair skies		❏ extra	❏ how come
❏ fall		❏ freezing	❏ it's raining cats and dogs
❏ hiking		❏ incredible	
❏ showers		❏ muddy	
❏ spring		❏ overnight	
❏ summer		❏ partly cloudy	
❏ weather forecast		❏ scared	
❏ winter		❏ sick of (verb + -ing)	

Check the things you did in this chapter. How well can you do each one?

	Very well	Fairly well	Not very well
I can listen to and practice stress and reductions.	❏	❏	❏
I can hear the difference between *can* and *can't*.	❏	❏	❏
I can talk about my abilities.	❏	❏	❏
I can take notes on a story.	❏	❏	❏
I can summarize my notes.	❏	❏	❏
I can guess meanings from context.	❏	❏	❏
I can talk about weather.	❏	❏	❏
I can talk about what I like to do.	❏	❏	❏

Write about what you learned and liked in this chapter.

In this chapter,

I learned _____

_____

I liked _____

_____

Living to Eat, or Eating to Live?

In This Chapter

Conversation: Shopping for Food

Advice Show: Healthy Eating

Getting Meaning from Context: In a Restaurant

Real-World Tasks: Following Recipes

> ❝ Tomatoes and oregano make it Italian; wine and tarragon make it French. Sour cream makes it Russian; lemon and cinnamon make it Greek. Soy sauce makes it Chinese; garlic makes it good. ❞
>
> —Alice May Brock
> American author (1941–)

Connecting to the Topic

1 Look at the photo. What are the people doing? What is their relationship to one another?

2 What are some of your favorite things to eat when you visit your family?

3 Eating lots of vegetables is healthy. What are three other healthy eating habits?

Before You Listen

 1 Prelistening Questions Look at the photo. Answer the questions with a partner.

▲ Andrew and Nancy at the supermarket

1. The supermarket in the picture has an "express line." What do you think this means?

2. There is a couple at the front of the line. What are they buying? What mistake do they make?

2 Previewing Vocabulary Listen to these words and phrases from the conversation. Then complete the sentences with the words and phrases.

Nouns		Verb	Expression
aisle	produce	take checks	in line
groceries	quart[2]		
pound[1]	tofu[3]		

1. Cherries are pretty cheap now. They cost $1.89 a _____.

2. My son likes milk a lot. He drinks a _____ of milk every day.

3. You can pay with cash or a credit card, but this market doesn't

   _____.

4. I hate frozen or canned vegetables and fruit. I only eat fresh

   _____.

5. I just spent $90.00 on _____. Last time I spent $85.00. Food is really expensive here!

6. **A:** Excuse me, where is the bread?

   B: It's in _____ four.

7. The market was very crowded. I had to wait _____ for 15 minutes to pay.

8. People who don't eat meat often cook with _____.

Listen

3 Listening for Main Ideas Andrew and Nancy are grocery shopping at a supermarket. Close your book as you listen. Prepare to answer these questions.

1. What are Andrew and Nancy discussing?

2. Why is Andrew buying so much food?

3. Why can't Andrew and Nancy use the express line?

Compare and discuss your answers with a partner.

4 Listening for Details Listen again if necessary. Write *T* if a statement is true and *F* if it is false.

_____ **1.** Andrew forgot to get tofu.

_____ **2.** Nancy wants Andrew to buy more ice cream.

_____ **3.** Strawberries cost $2.89.

---

[1] 2.2 pounds equal one kilogram.
[2] A quart is equal to about a liter.
[3] Tofu is a soft white food made from soy beans, popular in Asian cooking.

Stress

5 **Listening for Stressed Words** Listen to the conversation again. Some of the stressed words are missing. During each pause, repeat the phrase or sentence. Then fill in the blanks with words you hear.

Andrew: Well, I got a few groceries that _____ on the list.

Nancy: I can _____ that! We're _____ shopping for an _____, you know.

Andrew: I _____ do this when I'm hungry.

Nancy: Well, let's see what you _____ here.

Andrew: Some nice, fresh _____ for only _____ a pound.

Nancy: Well, that's fine. They always have nice _____ here. But _____ do you have all these _____?

Andrew: Don't you _____ them?

Nancy: Oh, I don't know . . . I hope you got a _____ of _____.

Andrew: I think I _____. Where's the _____ with the Asian foods, again?

Nancy: Aisle _____.

Andrew: I'll go get it.

Nancy: _____—this _____ you got looks really _____!

Andrew: Well, it _____. It's on _____ for just _____ a pound.

Nancy: And what's this? More ice cream? We already have a _____ at home. Why don't you put it _____? Meanwhile, I'll get in _____ right here.

Cashier: I'm _____, Miss; this is the _____ line, and it looks like you've got more than _____ items. Oh, and we don't take _____ here.

Now read the conversation with two other classmates. Practice stressing words correctly.

Reductions

6 Comparing Unreduced and Reduced Pronunciation The following sentences come from the conversation. Listen for the difference between unreduced and reduced pronunciation. Repeat both forms after the speaker.

Unreduced Pronunciation	Reduced Pronunciation*
1. Let's see what you have here.	Let's see whatcha have here.
2. Why do you have all these cookies	Why d'ya have all these cookies?
3. Don't you like them?	Dontcha like 'em?
4. I don't know.	I dunno.

7 Listening for Reductions Listen to the following sentences. You'll hear the reduced pronunciations of some words. Repeat each sentence during the pause. Then write the unreduced forms of the missing words in the blanks.

Customer: Waiter?

Server: Yes, sir. Do you know _____ _____ want?

Customer: _____ _____ have the spaghetti with mushroom sauce tonight?

Server: Yes, we do.

Customer: Well, are the mushrooms fresh or canned?

Server: They're fresh, and the sauce has _____

_____ them.

Customer: Great, I'll have that.

Server: _____ _____ want something to drink?

Customer: I _____ _____. Why _____

_____ recommend something?

Server: How about some nice Italian mineral water?

With a partner, repeat the sentences for pronunciation practice. Practice reduced pronunciation.

_____

* Note: The underlined forms are not acceptable spellings in written English.

After You Listen

8 Using Vocabulary Discuss the following questions with a partner. Use the underlined vocabulary in your answers.

1. Who shops for <u>groceries</u> in your family? How often?

2. What kinds of <u>produce</u> do you buy every week?

3. How much does a gallon (four <u>quarts</u> = about 4 liters) of gasoline cost right now? Recently, has this price gone up, gone down, or stayed the same?

4. Which of the following places do you think usually <u>take checks</u>: restaurants, supermarkets, department stores, car dealers, or movie theaters?

5. In your favorite food market, how many <u>aisles</u> are there?

6. About how many <u>pounds</u> (1 pound = about 1/2 kilogram) of groceries can you carry?

7. How do you feel when you have to stand <u>in line</u> for a long time?

Pronunciation

TEENS OR TENS?

Notice the differences in stress between the following pairs of words. In the numbers 13 to 19, be sure to stress the "-teen" ending. For 20, 30, 40, etc., to 90, stress the first syllable only. Listen.

thirteen	thirty
fourteen	forty
fifteen	fifty
sixteen	sixty
seventeen	seventy
eighteen	eighty
nineteen	ninety

9 Distinguishing Between Teens and Tens Listen to the sentences and circle the number you hear.

1. 13   30   **5.** 17   70

2. 14   40   **6.** 18   80

3. 15   50   **7.** 19   90

4. 16   60

10 **Listening for Teens and Tens** Listen to these sentences. Write the number you hear on the blank line in each picture.

1.

2.

3.

4.

5.

6.

7.

8.

9.

10.

Talk It Over

11 Interview Use count and noncount nouns as you interview people about food and shopping habits.

1. Work in groups of three. Write your teacher's name and the names of your group members in the spaces at the top of the chart below.

2. Ask questions with "How much" or "How many" and the words on the left side of the chart. Look at the example (Stacy).

Example
  A: How much coffee do you drink every day?
  B: Two cups a day.
  A: How many candy bars do you buy a week?
  B: Two a week.

3. Practice asking your teacher the questions and write his or her answers on the chart.

  ■ Use the present tense.
  ■ Pay attention to count and noncount nouns.
  ■ Add time expressions as needed. For example, "How much coffee do you drink *every week*?"

4. Take turns asking your group members the questions and write their answers on the chart.

Time Expressions you can use in the questions or answers:

each	day
every	week
a	month

Questions		Teacher	Name	Name
	Stacy			
coffee/drink	*2 cups a day*			
water/drink	*6 glasses a day*			
candy/buy	*2*			
food/eat/breakfast	*Only a little*			
money/spend/groceries	*About 30 dollars*			
gasoline/buy	*About 15 gallons*			
bananas/eat	*3 or 4*			
times/eat/restaurants	*8 or 9*			

Before You Listen

1 Prelistening Questions In the United States, people learn that they should eat food from the four major food groups: grains (wheat, corn, rice, etc.), fruits and vegetables, dairy (milk, cheese, yogurt, etc.), and protein (meat, fish, beans, nuts, eggs, etc.). Before you listen, answer these questions with a partner.

1. Talk about the photo. Are these young men "healthy" eaters?

2. Do you eat like these young men? For example, do you like "junk food"? If yes, what is your favorite type? If not, what kinds of food do you like to eat?

3. Do you ever eat canned or frozen food? Why or why not? If you *do* eat such foods, what are some examples?

4. Have you ever changed your eating habits (what, how much, or when you eat)? Explain how, and why, you changed.

2 Previewing Vocabulary You will hear the underlined words below on a radio advice show. Listen to the underlined words. Then write the letter of the correct definition beside each sentence.

Sentences

1. _____ Milk is a good <u>source</u> of calcium.

2. _____ We can get most <u>vitamins and minerals</u> from food. We don't have to take pills.

3. _____ If you start to <u>gain</u> weight, you are probably eating more food than your body needs.

4. _____ If you <u>skip</u> breakfast, you'll be really hungry by lunchtime.

5. _____ Dentists try to teach children good brushing and eating habits so they won't get tooth <u>decay</u>.

6. _____ The doctor told John to <u>cut down on</u> coffee, to help him sleep better.

7. _____ A piece of bread has about 75 <u>calories</u>.

8. _____ <u>Fiber</u> helps food move through our bodies easily.

Definitions

a. weakening, rotting

b. a unit for measuring the energy value of food

c. to reduce or have less of (something)

d. a food substance that comes from plants and that we need for digestion

e. helpful elements in many foods that are used by our bodies to grow and stay healthy

f. not to do or have something

g. a place where something comes from

h. to increase

Listen

 3 Listening for Main Ideas Listen to advice from a radio show called, "Eating Right!" As you listen, answer this question:

What are some important things you can do to eat right?

4 Taking Notes on Specific Information Listen again. This time, complete the chart with Bob and Pam's advice. Try to catch as many details as you can.

Things You Should Eat	Reasons	Examples
vegetables	fiber,	carrots,

Things You Shouldn't Eat or Drink	Reasons	Examples

After You Listen

5 Summarizing Ideas

1. Compare notes with a partner. Together, summarize in complete sentences the advice you heard. Include reasons and examples. Tell your partner if you have tried any of these ideas for healthy eating.

Example

You should eat a carrot for a snack because it's a vegetable that has . . .

2. With your class, make a list on the board of additional dos and don'ts about healthy eating. Tell the class which ones you have tried and if they worked well.

6 **Using Vocabulary** Discuss the following questions with a partner. Use the underlined vocabulary in your answers.

1. Which meal are you least likely to <u>skip</u>, and which meal are you most likely to <u>skip</u>? Why?

2. Bodybuilders, football players, and other athletes often try to <u>gain</u> weight and strength. What specific types of food would you suggest for these people to eat?

3. What do you eat or drink that you know may be bad for your teeth? Would you consider stopping? Would you <u>cut down on</u> these things? How do you try to avoid tooth <u>decay</u>?

4. Do you ever think about the number of <u>calories</u> in certain foods you eat? Do you read food labels? Why, or why not?

5. Which of your favorite foods do you think are the best <u>sources</u> of <u>vitamins</u> and <u>minerals</u>?

6. What kinds of foods do you eat to get <u>fiber</u> in your diet?

Talk It Over

7 **Comparing Eating Habits** "Eating habits" are your eating customs. They include when, where, and what you eat. Take notes in the chart below. Then use the chart to talk about differences between your eating habits at home and the way you eat when you travel somewhere.

	When I'm at Home	When I Travel
1. what you eat for breakfast, lunch, and dinner	I eat rice for breakfast.	I eat cereal for breakfast.
2. the time and size of meals and snacks		
3. the price of food		
4. restaurants		
5. table manners		

Getting Meaning from Context

1 Prelistening Questions Look at the photos. Each one shows a different kind of eating place. Before you listen, answer the questions on page 53 with a partner.

▲ A restaurant

▲ A cafeteria

▲ A fast food restaurant

▲ A diner

1. What kind of food does each place serve?

2. Who serves the food in each place?

3. Which one is probably the most expensive? The cheapest?

4. When would you choose to eat in each kind of place?

5. Which of these kinds of places have you tried?

6. What are some other types of places to eat?

Focus on Testing

Using Context Clues

Many tests such as the TOEFL® iBT measure your academic listening and speaking abilities. This activity, and others in the book, will develop your social and academic communication abilities, and provide a foundation for success on a variety of standardized tests. You will hear four conversations about places to eat.

1. Listen to the beginning of each conversation.

2. Listen to the question for each conversation. Stop the recording and choose the best answer to each question.

3. In the **Clues** column, write the words that helped you choose your answer.

4. Listen to the last part of each conversation to hear the correct answer.

Answers	Clues
1. (A) coffee shop (B) cafeteria (C) nice restaurant	
2. (A) fast-food place (B) diner (C) expensive restaurant	
3. (A) cafeteria (B) coffeehouse (C) fast-food place	
4. (A) nice restaurant (B) cafeteria (C) fast-food place	

ORDERING IN A RESTAURANT

In the United States, you can order dinner *à la carte,* which means you pay separately for each item. You can also order a complete dinner, which includes a main course (fish, meat, or a vegetarian dish), soup or salad, and side dishes (rice, potatoes, or vegetables) for one price. Drinks and dessert are usually separate. A "dish" in this context is a serving of cooked food, not a container.

Here is a list of questions and answers that are frequently used in restaurants.

Server	Customer
Taking an order:	*Ordering:*
Are you ready to order?	I'll have (the beans and rice).
May I take your order?	I'd like (a steak).
Do you want (an appetizer)?	May I please have (a glass of iced tea)?
Would you like (soup) or (salad)?	
Would you prefer (French fries) or (a baked potato)?	*Asking for information:*
	Do you have (tofu)?
What would you like (to drink)?	What kind of (salad dressing) do you have?
	Does that come with (a vegetable)?

2 Ordering in a Restaurant A customer is ordering a meal at a nice restaurant. Listen to the conversation.

Server: Are you ready to order, ma'am?
Customer: Yes, I am.
Server: What would you like?
Customer: I'd like the grilled salmon dinner.
Server: Would you like soup or salad with that?
Customer: What kind of soup do you have?
Server: We have Japanese miso soup or Italian minestrone.
Customer: I'll have the minestrone.
Server: And would you like potatoes or rice with your salmon?
Customer: Rice, please. Does the dinner come with a vegetable?
Server: Yes. Would you prefer green beans or broccoli?
Customer: Green beans, please.
Server: What would you like to drink?
Customer: I'd like a glass of iced tea.
Server: OK, that's minestrone soup, followed by grilled salmon with rice and green beans, and a glass of iced tea. Would you like an appetizer while you're waiting?
Customer: No thanks.

Now use the model above to role-play ordering dinner. Sit with a partner. One of you is the server. The other is a customer. Follow the instructions in the boxes below.

Server's Instructions

Start by asking the customer, "May I take your order?"

Then take the customer's order for a main course, soup or salad, side dishes, dessert, and a drink.

Customer's Instructions

Order the following items from the menu:

a main course	dessert
soup or salad	a drink
a side dish	

Ask questions about each course.

For example, "What kind of juice do you have?" "Is the shrimp fresh?"

DINNER MENU

SOUPS

Soup of the Day $3.25
Cheese Soup 3.50
Homemade Chili 3.75

SALADS

American Chef $7.25
Garden greens with turkey, ham, cheese

Golden Gate 7.75
Fresh pineapple stuffed with almond chicken salad

Tutti–Fruiti 7.75
Fresh fruits served with cottage cheese

SIDE ORDERS

French Fries $3.50

Mushrooms 4.25
Covered in cheese sauce

Mixed Vegetables 4.25
Steamed or stir-fried

HOUSE SPECIALTIES

All entrees served with your choice of rice, cottage cheese, tossed salad, choice of potato, roll and butter

Ribeye Steak $15.75
Grilled to order

Whole Chicken 14.75
Broiled, baked, or fried

Sesame Tofu 13.95
Sautéed with snow peas and scallions

Fantail Shrimp 17.95
Broiled with butter and lemon, or deep fried

DESSERTS

Apple Pie $4.75
Plenty of cinnamon and a scoop of ice cream

Ice Cream 3.75
Or your choice of low-fat yogurt

BEVERAGES

Fresh juices $2.50
Cola & Diet Cola 1.20
Milk 1.50

Recipes

1 **Previewing Vocabulary** The following words are used in cooking. Before you
listen, write the definitions of the words.

ingredients: _____

serve: _____

beat: _____

melt: _____

dip: _____

fry: _____

2 **Taking Notes on a Recipe** Tom is teaching Kenji how to cook French toast.
Listen to the recipe and take notes in the spaces.

Ingredients:

_____

_____

_____

_____

_____

Culture Note

Cooking Measurements
The measurements used in cooking in the U.S. are different from the
measurements used in other countries.
For example:

U.S.	Other Countries
a teaspoon	= 5 ml (milliliters)
a tablespoon	= 15 ml
a cup	= 240 ml

1.   2.   3.

Steps:
  1. Beat _____
  2. Melt _____
  3. Dip _____

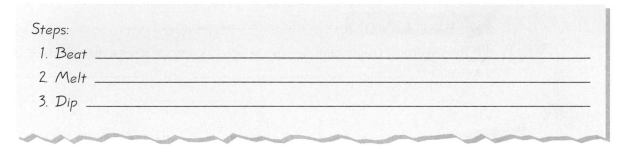

4.   5.

4. Fry _____
5. Serve _____

3 Explaining a Recipe Now, with a partner, use your notes to take turns explaining how to make French toast.

4 Sharing Recipes Teach the class a simple recipe for a dish that you know how to cook.

1. First, list the ingredients.

2. Then, describe each step (you may even try to demonstrate). As you speak, the class should take notes on the ingredients and steps.

3. Then, choose one or two people to retell the recipe using their notes.

Regional Foods

5 Prelistening Questions Before you listen, talk about "foreign" foods with a partner.

▲ Sushi

▲ Enchiladas with rice and beans

1. Do you know of any regions or places famous for special kinds of food? Give examples, and try to describe those foods.

2. Can you name some "foreign" foods and the countries they come from? Which foreign dishes have you tasted? What is your favorite?

3. Have you tried any North American food? What have you tried?

6 Regional Foods Andrew and Nancy plan to drive around the United States and Canada. Their friend, Paula, is a chef. She tells them about foods and drinks that are popular in different regions. Look at the map of the United States and Canada. As you hear the name of each food, write it on the map in the place where it is popular.

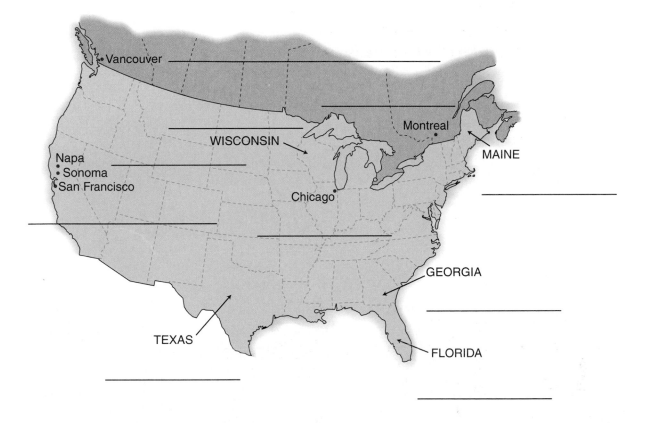

Discuss these questions with a partner.

1. Have you visited any of the cities or states mentioned by Paula? Did you eat any of the foods mentioned?

2. Which of the foods that Paula mentions would you like to try?

Talk It Over

7 Refusing Food Politely

1. Read the situation in the box below and answer the question.

Has something like this ever happened to you?

> A Korean student, Soo Yun, is having dinner at the home of her American friend, Cathy. Soo Yun has only eaten American food a few times before. During the meal, Cathy's mother offers Soo Yun some unfamiliar food. Soo Yun prefers not to eat it, but she doesn't want to be rude. What can she do?

2. Prepare the conversation between Soo Yun and Cathy's mother with a partner. Put on a skit for the class. You can use the expressions below. After each skit, discuss whether or not the food was refused politely.

Offering Food to Someone	Refusing Food Politely
Would you like some _____?	Thanks, but I'm getting full.
Would you like to try some _____?	Thanks, but I've had enough.
Why don't you have some (more) _____?	I'm really full, thanks.
Have some (more) _____.	It's delicious, but I really can't eat any more.
	It looks wonderful, but I can't eat any more.

Self-Assessment Log

Check the words you learned in this chapter.

Nouns

❑ aisle
❑ calories
❑ decay
❑ fiber
❑ groceries
❑ ingredients

❑ pound
❑ produce
❑ quart
❑ source
❑ tofu
❑ vitamins and minerals

Verbs

❑ beat
❑ cut down on
❑ dip
❑ fry
❑ gain
❑ melt
❑ serve
❑ skip
❑ take checks

Expressions

❑ in line

Check the things you did in this chapter. How well can you do each one?

	Very well	Fairly well	Not very well
I can listen to and practice stress and reductions.	❑	❑	❑
I can hear the difference between tens and teens.	❑	❑	❑
I can talk about food, recipes, and eating habits.	❑	❑	❑
I can take notes on a radio advice show.	❑	❑	❑
I can summarize my notes.	❑	❑	❑
I can guess meanings from context.	❑	❑	❑
I can order food from a menu.	❑	❑	❑

Write about what you learned and liked in this chapter.

In this chapter,

I learned _____

_____

I liked _____

_____

Chapter

4

In the Community

In This Chapter

Conversation: In the City

Conversation: Comparing Cities and Towns

Getting Meaning from Context: In the Community

Real-World Tasks: Asking for and Giving Directions

❝ A community is like a ship; everyone ought to be prepared to take the helm. **❞**

—Henrik Ibsen
Norwegian playwright (1828–1906)

Connecting to the Topic

1 Look at the photo. Where are these people? What are they doing?

2 Grocery shopping and doing laundry are examples of errands and chores. What kinds of errands and chores do you usually do each week?

3 What do you like and dislike most about your community?

Before You Listen

 1 Prelistening Questions Before you listen, talk about your community with a partner.

1. Where do you go to do the following?

   get cash   pay a traffic ticket   repair your computer

   clean your dirty clothes   buy medicine

2. Can you walk to these places from your home? If not, how do you get there?

3. Look at the photo. What is happening? What is the police officer going to do? Why?

▲ The police officer wants to speak to Kenji.

2 Previewing Vocabulary Listen to these words and phrases from the conversation. Then complete the sentences below with the words and phrases.

Words and Phrases	Definitions
give (someone) a ride	to take someone in your car
run errands	to take short trips to stores or other places of business
drop off (something/someone)	to take something or someone to a place
dry cleaner	a place where clothes are cleaned with chemicals, not water
laundry	clothes that need to be washed
convenient	comfortable and easy
debit card	a plastic card used to get money from a bank machine
have got to	must
jaywalking	crossing a street illegally

1. I have to _____ this afternoon. I have to go to the bank, mail a package, and go grocery shopping.

2. Most teenagers don't know how to do _____; their mothers or fathers usually wash their clothes for them.

3. It's very _____ to have a bus stop in front of my house. I can be at the bus stop in 30 seconds.

4. My car doesn't work and I need to be at my job in 30 minutes. Can you

   _____ me _____?

5. I'm sorry, I can't talk to you right now. My class starts in five minutes.

   I _____ go.

6. You can't wash your beautiful new jacket in a washing machine. You need to

   take it to the _____.

7. Most supermarkets let you pay with a credit card or a _____.

8. David _____ his daughter at school every morning and picks her up every afternoon.

9. I got a ticket for _____ yesterday. A police officer stopped me when I crossed in the middle of the street. From now on, I'll cross at the corner.

3 **Listening for Main Ideas** Peter and Kenji both plan to go downtown. Close your book as you listen to the conversation. Listen for the answers to these questions.

1. What does Kenji ask Peter to do?

2. What does Kenji need to do downtown?

3. Why is Peter going downtown?

Compare and discuss your answers with a partner.

4 **Listening for Details** Listen again if necessary. Write *T* if a statement is true and *F* if it is false.

_____ 1. Kenji needs to buy a new computer.

_____ 2. Both Peter and Kenji got a ticket.

_____ 3. Peter and Kenji can do laundry in their building.

Stress

5 **Listening for Stressed Words** Listen to the conversation again. Some of the stressed words are missing. During each pause, repeat the phrase or sentence. Then fill in the blanks with words you hear.

Kenji: Peter, are you going _____ today?

Peter: Uh-huh. Why?

Kenji: Can you _____ me a _____? I have to run

some _____.

Peter: Where do you need to _____?

Kenji: Uh, a lot of places. First, I have to go to the _____. Could

you drop me _____ at the _____ of King

Boulevard and Second Avenue?

Peter: King and Second? Oh, sure. I know where that is. But

_____ are you going to the _____? Why

don't you use the _____ machine on _____?

Kenji: 'Cause my _____ card isn't working; I've

_____ to get a _____ one. And the

_____ is next _____ to the bank. I have to

pick up some _____ there anyway.

Peter: Why don't you _____ the _____ room here

in the building?

Kenji: I'm not picking up laundry. It's dry cleaning. By the way, is there a

computer _____ shop near there? I need to drop off my

_____.

Peter: Computer _____? Oh, yeah. There's a Good Buy across

the _____ from the bank. They fix computers there.

Kenji: Oh, that's _____. So what are you going to do downtown?

Peter: I'm going to the _____. I've got to pay a

_____ ticket.

Kenji: No kidding! I have to pay a ticket, too. I just got a _____

last week.

Peter: But, Kenji, you don't _____!

Kenji: I know. I got a ticket for _____!

Peter: Really?!

Kenji: Yeah. I _____ know it's illegal to cross in the

_____ of the street!

Now read the conversation with two other classmates. Practice stressing words correctly.

Reductions

6 **Comparing Unreduced and Reduced Pronunciation** The following
sentences come from the conversation. Listen for the difference between unreduced
and reduced pronunciation. Repeat both forms after the speaker.

Unreduced Pronunciation	**Reduced Pronunciation***
1. Can you give me a ride?	Kinya gimme a ride?
2. Where do you need to go?	Where d'ya need ta go?
3. I have to run some errands	I hafta run some errands.
4. I've got to pay a traffic ticket.	I've gotta pay a traffic ticket.
5. Could you drop me off?	Couldja drop me off?
6. A lot of places.	A lotta places.
7. What are you going to do downtown?	What arya gonna do downtown?

_____

* Note: The underlined forms are not acceptable spellings in written English.

7 Listening for Reductions Listen to the following conversation. You'll hear the reduced pronunciations of some words. Repeat each sentence during the pause. Then write the unreduced forms of the missing words in the blanks.

A: _____ _____ know where Central Library is?

B: Sure. You _____ _____ take Bus number 9.

A: _____ _____ walk with me to the bus stop?

B: I'm sorry. I don't have time 'cause I've _____ _____ do a _____ _____ things.

A: Oh. Then _____ _____ just _____ _____ directions to the bus stop?

B: _____ _____ kidding? It's right there across the street.

With a partner, read the conversation. Practice reduced pronunciation.

8 Reductions Game Imagine that a big storm is coming to your area. You have ten minutes to leave your home and go to a safe place. Follow the steps to tell what you are going to do:

1. Work in a small group. Sit in a circle. The first student says one thing he or she is going to do. Use the reduced forms and the words from the Word Bank section in the box on page 69.

Example
Student 1:   I'm <u>gonna</u> rescue my cat.

2. The next student repeats the first student's sentence and then adds his or her own sentence.

Example
Student 2:   She's <u>gonna</u> rescue her cat. And I <u>hafta</u> find my medicine.

3. The third student repeats the first two sentences and adds his or her own, and so on. Continue around the group until someone can't remember all of the sentences.

Example
Student 3:   She's <u>gonna</u> rescue her cat. He <u>hasta</u> find his medicine. And I <u>wanna</u> call my brother.

4. The student who can remember all the sentences is the winner.

Reductions

have to	<u>hafta</u>
has to	<u>hasta</u>
going to	<u>gonna</u>
want to	<u>wanna</u>
got to	<u>gotta</u>
because	<u>'cause</u>

Word Bank

Nouns	Verbs
brother/sister	call
clothes	find
family photos	look for
jewelry	rescue
medicine	save
money	take
my cat/dog	turn off the gas
TV	

After You Listen

9 **Using Vocabulary** Discuss the following questions with a partner. Use the underlined vocabulary in your answers.

1. Do you ever <u>drop</u> anything <u>off</u> anywhere before school or after school? Explain.

2. How do you get to school? Do you drive, take a bus, or does someone <u>drop you off</u>?

3. Who does <u>the laundry</u> in your family? When you travel, do you do your own laundry or do you use the hotel's laundry service? Which clothes do you take to a <u>dry cleaner</u>?

4. Name some <u>errands</u> that you have to <u>run</u> this week. What type of transportation will you use to run your errands?

5. Is it a good idea to <u>give</u> a stranger <u>a ride</u>? Why or why not?

6. Is the place where you live now <u>convenient</u>? For example, is there good transportation nearby? Can you walk to a market easily?

7. What are some things you <u>have got to</u> do before you go to bed tonight?

8. Explain the difference between a credit card and a <u>debit card</u>.

Using Language Functions

DESCRIBING LOCATIONS

Read Activity 5 on page 66 again. Find the location of the places where Kenji will go and write them in the blanks.

Bank: _____

Dry cleaner: _____

Computer repair shop: _____

Streets can be called *avenue, boulevard, road, drive*, or *way*. These words are very important when writing an exact address. They are not so important in giving directions.

Example

I live at 8051 Holloway Avenue. My house is at the corner of Holloway and Pacific.

The following expressions are often used to describe a location.

- on _____ (name of street)
- near
- nearby
- next to
- next door to
- in front of
- across from/across the street from
- at the corner of _____ and _____
- two/three/four blocks from
- in the middle of the block
- the second/third/fourth building from the corner

▲ Central Park in New York City is 50 blocks long.

10 Finding Locations Work with a partner. Read these sentences. Then look at the picture and decide if the locations are correct or incorrect. If the location is wrong, make the necessary correction. Use expressions on page 70.

Example The Copy Shop is in front of the medical building.
No, that's wrong. The Copy Shop is across the street from the medical building.

1. The ice cream truck is next to the medical building.
2. The bus station is the second building from the corner.
3. The park is near the bank.
4. The post office is next door to the department store.
5. The Copy Shop is in the middle of the block.
6. The ambulance is in front of the department store.

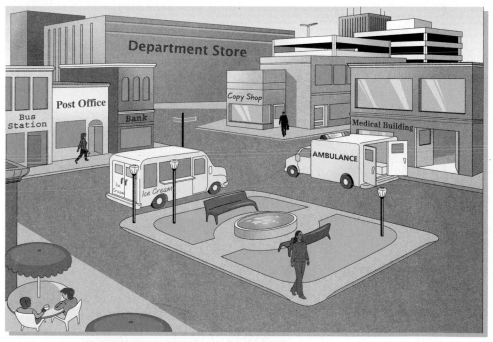

▲ A city neighborhood

11 Describing Your Neighborhood Describe your neighborhood to a partner. Use the expressions for describing locations.

Example My neighborhood is noisy but I like it. There is a movie theater nearby. It's just three blocks from my house. My place is also very convenient because . . .

Before You Listen

 1 Prelistening Questions You will hear a conversation about large and small communities. Before you listen, answer these questions with a partner.

1. Which photo looks most like your community?

2. Size is one difference between a village, a town, and a city. What other differences can you think of?

▲ A village

▲ A town

▲ A city

2 Previewing Vocabulary You will hear the underlined words below in a conversation. Listen to the underlined words. Then write the letter of the correct definition beside each sentence.

Sentences

1. _____ Do you know why the color of the sky is brown? It's the <u>smog</u> from all the cars and factories.

2. _____ I don't like to take the bus at 5:00 in the afternoon. It's always <u>crowded</u> with so many people coming home from work.

3. _____ Linda's grandmother is very <u>conservative</u> in her thinking; she doesn't like Linda to wear short dresses or to go out with boys before she is 18 years old.

4. _____ Winter in Canada is very cold, but there is also an <u>advantage</u>: there are great places to ski.

5. _____ Patrick wants to work in the United States. His big <u>disadvantage</u> is that he doesn't speak English.

Definitions

a. good thing, positive point

b. old-fashioned, traditional

c. bad thing, negative point

d. dirty air

e. full (of people)

Listen

3 Listening for Main Ideas Peter and Kenji just came back from downtown. They are talking to Ming about their trip. As you listen, decide what the main idea of the conversation is. Then answer the question below.

What is the best title for this conversation?
- (A) Kenji and Peter's Big City Adventure
- (B) Small Towns Are Better Than Big Cities
- (C) Why Small Towns Are Better for Girls
- (D) No Place Is Perfect

Discuss your choice with your classmates. Tell why you think the other titles don't show the main idea.

▲ Peter

▲ Kenji

▲ Ming

Strategy

Graphic Organizer: Concept Map

A concept map can help you organize your notes when a speaker is comparing two or more sides of a topic. You can also use a concept map to organize your own ideas when you are making this kind of comparison.

4 **Taking Notes on Specific Information** Listen again. As you listen, write the key words about big cities and small towns.

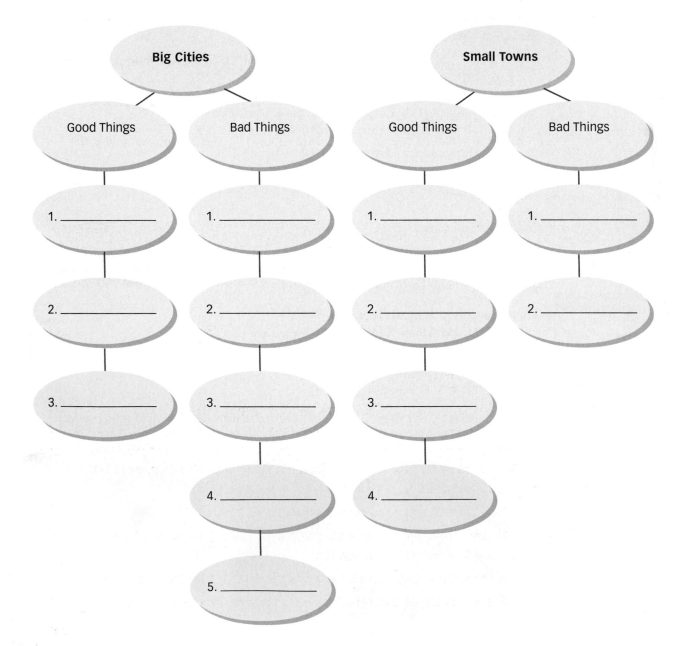

5 Summarizing Ideas Compare your notes with a partner. Using the key words from Activity 4, form complete sentences about what Peter, Kenji, and Ming said.

Example

They talked about three advantages of big cities. First, cities are exciting. Also, there is good shopping there, and . . .

6 Using Vocabulary Discuss your answers to the following questions with a partner. Use the underlined vocabulary in your answers.

1. Is there a lot of smog in the community where you live now? What is your government doing to reduce smog?

2. Name some times and places that are crowded in the city. How do you feel in a crowded place?

3. Who is the most conservative in your family? What are they conservative about: clothes? music? education? politics?

4. Name some advantages and disadvantages of driving to work and taking the subway to work.

Part 3 Strategies for Better Listening and Speaking

Getting Meaning from Context

TOEFL® iBT

Focus on Testing

Using Context Clues Many tests such as the TOEFL® iBT measure your academic listening and speaking abilities. This activity, and others in the book, will help develop your social and academic communication abilities and provide a foundation for success on a variety of standardized tests. You are going to hear five conversations from different parts of the city.

1. Listen to the beginning of each conversation.

2. Listen to the question for each conversation. Stop the recording and choose the best answer to each question.

3. In the **Clues** column, write the words that helped you choose your answer.

4. Listen to the last part of each conversation to hear the correct answer.

Answers	Clues
1. (A) in a post office (B) in a bank (C) in a gas station	
2. (A) on a train (B) in a taxi (C) on a bus	
3. (A) at a clothing store (B) at a dry cleaner (C) at a coffee shop	
4. (A) getting a driver's license (B) visiting an eye doctor (C) taking a final exam	
5. (A) at an airport (B) at a bank (C) at a post office	

Talk It Over

1 Role-Play Mr. Kim was in a hurry to buy a birthday present. He parked his car on the street. When he finished shopping, he got a surprise!

1. With a partner, discuss the cartoon on the next page. Use the vocabulary in the box below to explain what is happening.

2. Then prepare and perform a conversation between Mr. Kim and the parking officer.

Expressions	Verbs	Nouns
Oh, no!	park	ticket/citation
I can't believe it!	tow away	law
What's going on?		tow truck
Give me a break, officer.		sign

Part 4   Real-World Tasks: Directions

Using Language Functions

EXPRESSIONS FOR ASKING FOR AND GIVING DIRECTIONS

You will listen to Peter getting directions to different places in the city. Before you listen, study the expressions listed below.

Asking for Directions	Giving Directions
Could you tell me where . . . is?	Go straight.
Where is . . . ?	Go straight **for** two blocks **on** (Lennox) Avenue/ Street/Road.
Do you know how to get to . . . ?	
How do I get to . . .	Go past (the market).
I'm looking for . . .	Go north/south/east/west.
I'm trying to find . . .	Turn right/left.
	Make a right/left.
	Cross the street.
	You'll see it on your right/left.

1 **Reading a Map** Look at the map below. Follow the way from the café to the tennis courts. Write the directions on the lines below.

Go north on Lennox.

_____

_____

_____

Now write directions from the tennis courts to the movie theater.

_____

_____

_____

_____

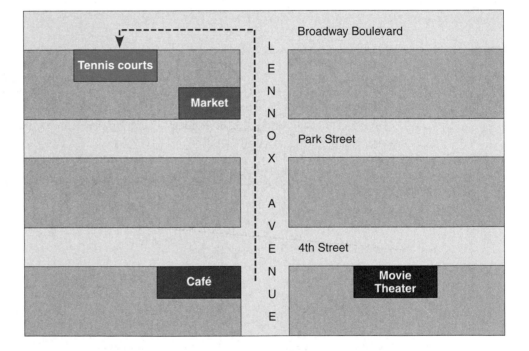

2 **Following Directions** Peter is getting directions to various places in the city. Right now, he is at Joe's Diner on Columbus Street.

1. Find Joe's Diner on the map below.

2. Listen to the directions and follow them on the map.

3. As you listen, write the name of each place that Peter is looking for on the map.

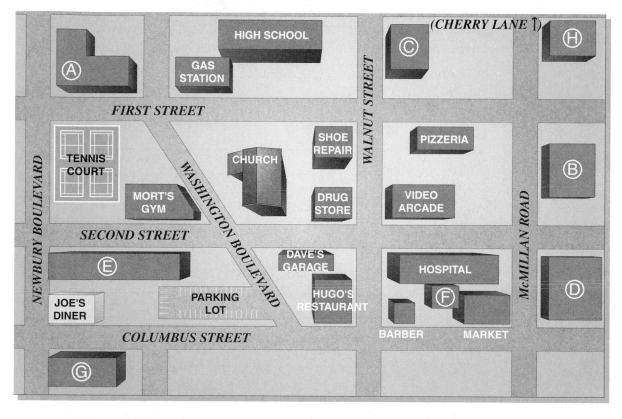

3 **Giving Directions** Look at the map above. Work with a partner. Ask for directions to the places listed below.

Example

A: How do I get from the hospital to the gas station?

B: Go north on Walnut, turn left on . . .

1. from the hospital to the gas station

2. from the parking lot to the high school

3. from the barbershop to Mort's Gym

4. from the tennis courts to the market

Choose one of these buildings on the map: A, B, D, or G, but don't tell your partner which one. Give directions to the building from Joe's Diner. Ask your partner to tell you the letter of the building that he or she arrives at.

GETTING DIRECTIONS ON THE PHONE

If you need directions, your local bus company can help you. Call the bus company and tell them:

- where you want to leave from
- where you want to go
- what time you need to get there

 4 **Listening for Directions on the Phone** Listen to the following telephone conversations with the Metro Bus Company. Take notes on each conversation.

1. Destination: _____

   Bus number: _____

   Time to get on: _____

   Place to get on: _____

   Place to get off: _____

2. Destination: _____

   Time to get on: _____

   Place to get on: _____

   Fare: $ _____

   Travel time: _____

3. Destination: _____

   Bus number: _____

   Place to get on: _____

   How often bus runs: _____

Compare your notes with a partner.

Language Tip
The word **fare** is used for the cost of transportation.
Example: How much is the **airfare** from Miami to Sao Paulo? I need $25 for **cab fare**. Do you have enough money for the **bus fare**?

▲ Which bus should I take?

Self-Assessment Log

Check the words you learned in this chapter.

Nouns	Verbs	Expressions
❏ advantage	❏ drop off	❏ conservative
❏ debit card	(something or	❏ convenient
❏ disadvantage	someone)	❏ crowded
❏ dry cleaner	❏ give (someone)	
❏ jaywalking	a ride	
❏ laundry	❏ have got to	
❏ smog	❏ run errands	

Check the things you did in this chapter. How well you can do each one?

	Very well	Fairly well	Not very well
I can listen to and practice stress and reductions.	❏	❏	❏
I can listen to, ask for, and give directions.	❏	❏	❏
I can take notes on a conversation.	❏	❏	❏
I can summarize my notes.	❏	❏	❏
I can guess meanings from context.	❏	❏	❏
I can talk about maps.	❏	❏	❏

Write what you learned and liked in this chapter.

In this chapter,

I learned _____

_____

I liked _____

_____

5

Home

❝ A good home must be made, not bought. ❞

—Joyce Maynard
American author,
(1953–)

Connecting to the Topic

1 What are the men in the picture doing? Why?

2 How many times in your life have you moved? What were the reasons?

3 Is it common for young adults in your culture to live by themselves? Why or why not?

Before You Listen

1 Prelistening Questions Before you listen, talk with a partner.

1. Look at the photo. What is happening?

2. What kind of place do you live in now: an apartment? a house? a student dormitory?

▲ Beth and an apartment manager (landlord)

2 Previewing Vocabulary Listen to the words and phrases from the conversation. Then complete the sentences below with the words and phrases.

Nouns	Verbs	Adjectives	Adverb
closet	move (in/out)	furnished/unfurnished	pretty
fireplace	raised	stressed out	
landlord			
studio			
vacancy			

1. Mr. Davis is the owner of the house where I live. He always helps me when something is broken in the kitchen or the bathroom. He is a very good

   _____ .

2. Don't leave your clothes and shoes in the living room. Put them in your

   _____ .

3. I only need one room to live in because I'm alone and I don't have much money. So I'm going to rent a _____ apartment.

4. Jack has to buy a bed, a desk, a table, chairs, and some other things because his new apartment is _____ .

5. My place is _____ close to campus. It's only a 20-minute walk.

6. After two years, the owner of the building I live in _____ my rent from $850 to $950 a month.

7. This hotel is full; it has no _____ . We'll have to look for a room at another hotel.

8. I like to use my _____ in winter. It makes my apartment warm and romantic.

9. If you don't like your apartment, you can _____ and find another place.

10. Joanne has to study for two tests tomorrow, and she also has to pick up her parents at the airport. That's why she feels _____ .

Listen

3 Listening for Main Ideas Ming is talking to her friend Beth about apartments. Close your books as you listen to the conversation. Listen for the answers to these questions.

1. Why is Beth stressed out?

2. What does Beth learn from Ming that makes Beth feel better?

Compare and discuss your answers with a partner.

4 Listening for Details Listen again if necessary. Write *T* if a statement is true and *F* if it is false.

_____ **1.** Ming's building is close to campus.

_____ **2.** Ming's building has a parking garage.

_____ **3.** In Ming's building, a one-bedroom apartment rented for $850 a month.

_____ **4.** Beth needs an unfurnished apartment.

Stress

5 Listening for Stressed Words Listen to the conversation again. Some of the stressed words are missing. During each pause, repeat the phrase or sentence. Then fill in the blanks with words you hear.

Beth: I'm _____ stressed _____. My landlord just raised my _____. I think I'll have to _____.

Ming: Really? You know, my building has some _____. It's a pretty nice place, and it's just _____ minutes from campus.

Beth: Oh yeah? How much is the rent for a _____?

Ming: There are no _____ apartments in our building. My neighbor just _____ _____ of a one-bedroom. He paid $850 a month, I think.

Beth: That's not _____. Tell me more.

Ming: Well, one-bedrooms come with a _____, a kitchen, a fireplace in the _____ room, pretty big closets, and uh . . . Are you looking for a _____ or unfurnished place?

Beth: Unfurnished. I have all my _____ stuff. What about parking and _____?

Ming: There's no garage. You have to park on the street. But there *is* a _____ room downstairs.

Beth: Hmm. I think I'm _____. Could you give me the address?

Ming: Sure. It's 1213 Rose Avenue. The _____ name is Mr. Azizi. Call him up or _____ _____ _____ and talk to him.

Beth: Thanks, Ming. I'm going to do that tomorrow for _____.

Now read the conversation with a partner. Practice stressing words correctly.

Reductions

6 **Comparing Unreduced and Reduced Pronunciation.** The following sentences come from the conversation. Listen for the difference between unreduced and reduced pronunciation. Repeat both forms after the speaker.

Unreduced Pronunciation	Reduced Pronunciation*
1. I think I'll have to move.	I think I'll <u>(h)afta</u> move.
2. Are you looking for a furnished place?	<u>Arya</u> looking for a furnished place?
3. You have to park on the street.	You <u>(h)afta</u> park on the street.
4. Could you give me the address?	<u>Couldja gimme</u> the address?
5. Call him up.	Call <u>'im</u> up.
6. Stop by and talk to him.	Stop by <u>'n'</u> talk to <u>'im</u>.
7. I'm going to do that tomorrow.	I'm <u>gonna</u> do that tomorrow.

Language Tip

Note that sometimes the **h** at the beginning of a word is reduced, and sometimes it isn't: You might hear, "I'll **hafta** move" (or) "I'll **afta** park."

7 **Listening for Reductions** Listen to the following conversation. You'll hear the reduced pronunciations of some words. Repeat each sentence during the pause. Then write the unreduced forms of the missing words in the blanks.

A: Mr. Azizi, I _____ _____ talk to you. I have another problem.

B: _____ _____ call me later? I'm busy now.

A: No, I need the plumber again. _____ _____ call _____ right now?

B: I have a _____ _____ things to do. I'll call _____ tomorrow morning, okay?

A: No, I need _____ right now!

B: _____ _____ having trouble with the toilet again?

A: Yes. Look, just _____ _____ the plumber's phone number. I'll call _____.

B: All right, all right. Just _____ _____ a minute and I'll do it.

With a partner, read the conversation. Practice reduced pronunciation.

---

* Note: The underlined forms are not acceptable spellings in written English.

After You Listen

8 **Using Vocabulary** Work in pairs. Student A should look at page 201. Student B should look at page 205. Follow the instructions. Study the information in your box for a few minutes before you begin.

Pronunciation

THE *-ED* ENDING IN PAST TENSE VERBS

The *-ed* ending in past tense verbs is pronounced one of three ways, depending on the sound that comes before *-ed*.

/id/ after *-d* and *-t*
Examples waited, invited, needed

/t/ after unvoiced sounds: *-p, -k, -f, -s, -ch, -sh, -x*
Examples missed, watched, helped

/d/ after vowels and other voiced sounds: *-b, -g, -j, -m, -n, -l, -r, -th, -v, -z, -w*
Examples lived, showed, listened

9 **Distinguishing Among -ed Endings** Listen and write the following words. Then check the sound you hear at the end of the word.

	/id/	/t/	/d/
1. _____turned_____	☐	☐	☑
2. _____	☐	☐	☐
3. _____	☐	☐	☐
4. _____	☐	☐	☐
5. _____	☐	☐	☐
6. _____	☐	☐	☐
7. _____	☐	☐	☐
8. _____	☐	☐	☐
9. _____	☐	☐	☐
10. _____	☐	☐	☐

10 **Pronouncing -ed Endings** Work with a partner. Ask and answer the following questions in complete sentences. Pay attention to the pronunciation of the *-ed* endings.

1. When did you <u>move</u> to the home, or place, you live in now?
2. Who <u>recommended</u> this school to you?
3. When did you first <u>start</u> cleaning or decorating your own childhood bedroom?
4. When was the last time you <u>called</u> your family?
5. What TV programs or movies did you <u>watch</u> at home, recently?

11 Using -ed Endings Working with a partner, look at the pictures. Talk about Jennifer's moving day. Use the past tense of each verb. Pronounce the -ed endings carefully.

Example

> Jennifer moved into her new place. First, the movers carried the boxes inside and Jennifer watched them. Then, Jennifer . . .

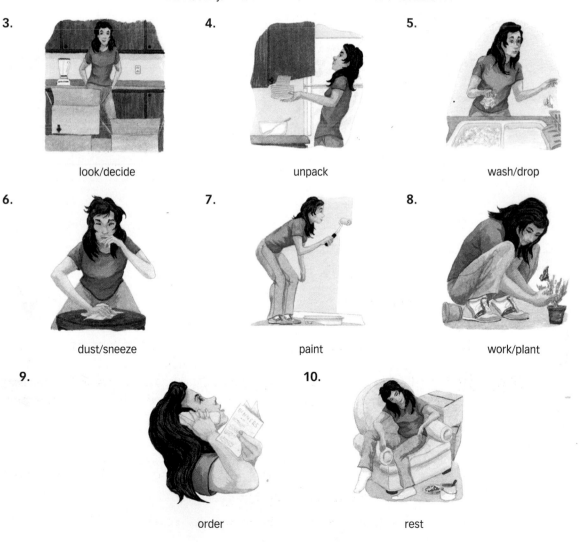

1.

move/carry/watch

2.

call/ask/describe

3.

look/decide

4.

unpack

5.

wash/drop

6.

dust/sneeze

7.

paint

8.

work/plant

9.

order

10.

rest

12 Asking for Information About Apartments

1. Look at the three apartment advertisements. They do not give very much information.

2. Make up five questions about the apartment in each ad. Use the ideas on the right.

3. Work with a partner. One of you is the manager, and the other one is the renter. Ask and answer the questions you prepared.

4. Change roles for each ad.

1.

> *Beautiful apartment;*
> *walk to campus.*
> *Call 555-2009 for more*
> *information.*

Rent? _____

_____

Number of rooms? _____

_____

Noise? _____

_____

Stove/refrigerator? _____

_____

(Your own question) _____

_____

2.

TWO-BEDROOM APARTMENT
$1500. Good location. Call 555–1828.

Area? _____

_____

Lease? _____

_____

Garage? _____

_____

Number of bathrooms? _____

_____

(Your own question) _____

_____

3.

ROOMMATE NEEDED
to share house. Lots of
privacy. Leave message
at **555-5520**.

Male/female? _____

_____

Number of rooms? _____

_____

Smoking? _____

_____

Location? _____

_____

Rent? _____

Part 2   Conversation: Touring an Apartment

Before You Listen

1 Prelistening Questions You will hear a conversation between Beth and an apartment manager showing her the apartment. Before you listen, answer these questions with a partner.

1. What do you like and dislike about the home where you live now? Name two good things and two bad things.

2. Who found your current home for you: you? your parents? a housing advisor? an agent?

3. In your experience, in what ways are apartment managers generally helpful or unhelpful?

2 Previewing Vocabulary Listen to the underlined words from the conversation. Then write the letter of the correct definition for each underlined word beside each sentence.

Sentences

1. _____ My apartment <u>lease</u> says that I have to stay there for one year.

2. _____ I need a new apartment. Is there an <u>available</u> apartment in your building?

3. _____ My shower is broken. Can you <u>fix</u> it?

4. _____ You don't have to sign a lease for this apartment. You can just rent it <u>month-to-month</u>.

5. _____ A pipe in my bathroom has a <u>leak</u>, and now my bathroom is full of water.

Definitions

a. able to be bought/rented/acquired

b. to repair; to make something work again

c. a crack or hole that allows liquid to escape

d. a contract; a signed agreement to live in a home for a period of time

e. without a yearly contract

3 **Listening for Main Ideas** Beth is looking at an apartment in Ming's building. Listen to her conversation with the manager. To help you remember the main points, take notes on these questions while you listen.

1. Which rooms is the manager showing Beth?

_____

2. Is this a good apartment or not?

_____

3. What's Beth's decision?

_____

_____

4 **Taking Notes on Specific Information** Listen again. Take more detailed notes about the good things and the bad things in the apartment. Compare your list with a partner.

Rooms Visited	Good Points	Bad Points
living room		
apartment in general		

After You Listen

5 **Summarizing Ideas** Compare notes with a partner. Together, summarize the conversation. As you speak, look at your notes from Activities 3 and 4 to help you remember.

6 Using Vocabulary Discuss the following questions with a partner. Use the underlined vocabulary in your answers.

1. What is the advantage of a <u>lease</u> for (a) the renter? (b) the landlord?

2. Why do some people prefer to rent a place <u>month-to-month</u> rather than for a whole year?

3. If anything breaks in your home, who <u>fixes</u> it?

4. If your friend is moving to a new house or apartment, what days are you <u>available</u> to help him or her?

5. If your ceiling has a <u>leak</u>, what should you do?

Using Language Functions

MAKING AND ANSWERING REQUESTS

It is important to learn how to make and answer formal and informal requests correctly.

	Making Requests	Answering Requests	
		Yes	**No**
Formal ↓	Could you . . .? Would you please . . .? Can you please . . .? Would you mind* _____ ing . . .?	Certainly. Of course. I would be happy to. I don't mind.*	I'm afraid I can't I'm sorry, I can't. I'm sorry, but that's impossible.
Informal (or stronger)	I'd like you to . . . I need you to . . . I want you to . . .	Sure. Okay. No problem.	Absolutely not.** No way.**
* "Would you mind . . .?" means "Is it a problem for you?" The answer is negative: "I don't mind" means "It's not a problem."			
** "Absolutely not" and "No way" are strong refusals which could be considered rude.			

 7 Role-Play Beth likes the apartment in Ming's building. However, she wants some of the "bad things" corrected. She decides to ask the manager about these things:

> changing the wall color   lowering the rent
> putting in air conditioning   having some pets
> fixing the bathroom leak

1. With a partner, role-play a conversation between Beth and Mr. Azizi, the manager. Use the expressions in the chart above.

2. After you practice, perform your role-plays for the class. Then talk about the levels of politeness that each pair used and how that possibly affected the results in each role-play.

Getting Meaning from Context

TOEFL® iBT

Focus on Testing

Using Context Clues Many tests such as the TOEFL® iBT measure your academic listening and speaking abilities. This activity, and others in the book, will develop your social and academic communication abilities, and provide a foundation for success on a variety of standardized tests. Listen to the following conversations between roommates.

1. Listen to the beginning of each conversation.

2. Listen to the question for each conversation. Stop the recording and choose the best answer to each question. Remember to use clues, signals, words you know, grammar, stress, and intonation to help you guess.

3. In the **Clues** column, write the words that helped you choose your answer.

4. Listen to the last part of each conversation to hear the correct answer.

Answers	Clues
1. (A) studied for an exam (B) had a party at the house (C) talked with a friend until 3:00 A.M.	
2. (A) because she is messy and doesn't clean (B) because she won't talk to her (C) because she doesn't take care of the furniture	
3. (A) they like the same television shows (B) they usually watch the news (C) there's only one television in the house	
4. (A) his roommate should pay more than half (B) his roommate uses the phone too much (C) his roommate should pay all the bills	
5. (A) it has four bedrooms (B) it's not comfortable for four people (C) the rent is shared by four roommates	

Talk It Over

1 **Finding a Roommate** Nabil and Roberto don't know each other. They meet at "Roommate Finders," because they are both looking for roommates. Read about Nabil and Roberto and decide if they will agree to be roommates.

> **Nabil**
> His rent just went up. To save money, he wants to share his apartment with someone. He is a very clean, quiet, and neat guy. He has a job and a cat.

> **Roberto**
> He wants to move out of his parents' home. He is looking for a cheap place to rent. He is messy and plays drums in a rock band. He has a part-time job and goes to school part-time. He has a small dog.

With a partner, prepare and perform a role-play between Nabil and Roberto.

Strategy

Graphic Organizer: Multi-Column Chart

A multi-column chart can help you keep track of things that you have to do. For example, you can use this kind of chart to plan your homework for the week. List your classes in the left column, the task you have for each class in the second column, how long each task will take, when you plan to do the task, and so on:

Classes	Tasks	How long will it take me?	When will I do it?
English	write a paragraph	two hours	Monday afternoon
Math	p. 46, Exercise A	one hour	Tuesday morning

1 Preparing to Leave Home for Vacation Before going on vacation, some people ask a friend or neighbor to take care of their home while they are gone.

1. Look at the list of items to take care of in the chart on the next page. Think about the things you or your family would need done if everyone left home for a month. Discuss the possibilities with a partner or in a small group.

2. Before Beth's uncle went away for a month-long vacation, he called to ask her to take care of his house while he was away. Listen to their conversation. Complete the chart to show what Beth's uncle wants her to do.

▲ Beth's uncle's house

Homecare Vacation Instructions			
Item to Take Care of	What to Do	How Often/When to Do It	Details, Notes
1. *mail* *newspaper*	a) b) *pick up from yard*		
2. *dog*	a) b) c)		*Dog food will be in bag in kitchen*
3. *garbage*	a)		*Uncle will take garbage to street*
4. *rose bushes*	a)		
5. *swimming pool and house*	a) *clean up*		

Listen again, then compare your chart with one or more classmates to try to complete the list accurately.

2 Listening to Moving Instructions Look at Beth's empty new apartment. She is going to tell the movers where to put each item.

1. Before you listen, look at the apartment and predict where the furniture and other things will go.

2. Now listen to Beth's instructions to the movers. Write the number of each thing in the correct place on the picture.

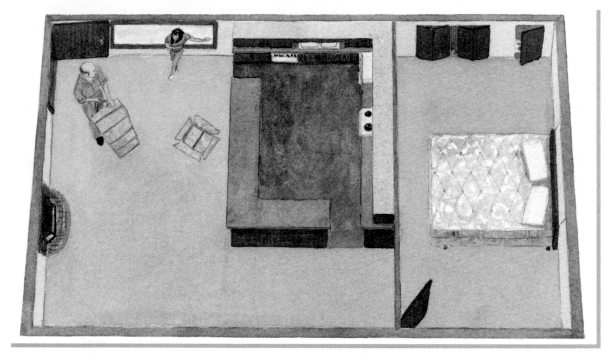

1.

2.

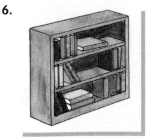

3.

4.

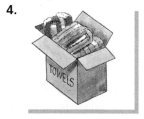

5.

6.

7.

3 Comparing Pictures Work in pairs. Student A should look at the picture on page 201. Student B should look at the picture on page 205. Tell each other about each item and its location in the room. Find ten differences without looking at each other's pictures.

Example

A: In my picture, there is a shoe beside the bed.
B: In mine, the shoe is in front of the closet.

Self-Assessment Log

Check the words you learned in this chapter.

Nouns	**Verbs**	**Adjectives**	**Adverbs**
❑ closet	❑ fix	❑ available	❑ pretty
❑ fireplace	❑ move (in/out)	❑ furnished/unfurnished	**Expressions**
❑ landlord	❑ raise	❑ stressed out	❑ month-to-month
❑ leak			
❑ lease			
❑ studio			
❑ vacancy			

Check the things you did in this chapter. How well can you do each one?

	Very well	Fairly well	Not very well
I can listen to and practice stress and reductions.	❑	❑	❑
I can listen to and pronounce *-ed* endings.	❑	❑	❑
I can talk about finding an apartment.	❑	❑	❑
I can take notes on a conversation.	❑	❑	❑
I can summarize my notes.	❑	❑	❑
I can make and answer requests.	❑	❑	❑
I can guess meanings from context.	❑	❑	❑
I can talk about homecare.	❑	❑	❑

Write what you learned and what you liked in this chapter.

In this chapter,

I learned _____

_____

I liked _____

_____

Chapter

6

Cultures of the World

In This Chapter

Conversation:	Learning New Customs
Lecture:	Coming-of-Age Ceremonies
Getting Meaning from Context:	Cultural Differences
Real-World Tasks:	Dining Customs

❝ No culture has a monopoly on beauty and no religion has a monopoly on truth. ❞

—Voltaire (François-Marie Arouet)
French writer and philosopher
(1694–1778)

Connecting to the Topic

1 Look at the photo. What is the young woman doing?

2 What kinds of difficulties can a person have when visiting or moving to a place with a different culture?

3 What places and cultures are you interested in? Why?

Before You Listen

 1 Prelistening Questions Before you listen, talk about travel with a partner.

▲ Salma talking on her cell phone.

1. Discuss the situation in the photo. Why shouldn't Salma use her cell phone?

2. Do you know the expression "When in Rome, do as the Romans do"? Tell about a time when you followed this advice.

3. How do you feel when you travel to a new place, meet new people, and experience new customs? Circle the words in the box that describe how you feel. Explain or give examples of times that you have had these feelings.

excited	careful	afraid	shy	nervous
energetic	homesick	worried	interested	curious

2 Previewing Vocabulary Listen to the underlined words. You will hear these words in the conversation. Then use the context to guess their meanings. Write your guesses in the spaces.

Contexts	Meanings
1. My first <u>impression</u> of my new boss was not good. He seemed strict and unfriendly when I first met him, but now I like him.	
2. I don't like getting up at 6 A.M., but I am <u>used to</u> it now because I've been doing it every day for three years.	
3. Mr. and Mrs. Haley like to travel to <u>exotic</u> places. They like unusual and interesting vacations.	
4. If you don't finish your food in an American restaurant, you can take the remaining food home in a <u>doggie bag</u>.	
5. When I arrived in the U.S., I was <u>amazed</u> by the number of large cars on the road. There were so many! We have only small cars where I'm from.	
6. Our teacher has not given us a lot of homework <u>so far</u>, but maybe she'll give us more next week.	
7. When we finished dinner, we saved the <u>leftovers</u> in the refrigerator.	

Listen

3 Listening for Main Ideas Kenji is having lunch with Yolanda and her friend Salma, who is visiting from Lebanon. Close your book as you listen to the conversation. Listen for the answers to these questions.

1. What is Salma's impression of the United States?

2. What surprised Salma in the restaurant?

Compare and discuss answers with a partner.

4 Listening for Details Listen again if necessary. Write *T* if a statement is true and *F* if it is false.

_____ **1.** Salma doesn't like hotdogs because they don't taste good.

_____ **2.** Kenji likes American food.

_____ **3.** At the Mexican restaurant, Yolanda was surprised when Salma asked for a doggie bag.

_____ **4.** In Salma's country, using cell phones is common everywhere.

_____ **5.** Salma says "When in Rome, do as the Romans do" to mean that she will start eating American food.

Stress

5 Listening for Stressed Words Listen to part of the conversation again. Some of the stressed words are missing. During each pause, repeat the phrase or sentence. Then fill in the blanks with the words you hear.

Kenji: So, Salma, is this your _____ trip to the United States?

Salma: Yes, it is.

Kenji: And what's your _____ so far?

Salma: Well, the people are really _____, and the city is beautiful. But the _____; well, it's not so good.

Kenji: Oh, yeah, that's what I thought too when I _____ got here. But I'm _____ to American food now. I actually _____ hotdogs and French fries.

Yolanda: So last night I took Salma to a _____ restaurant. I wanted her to try something _____.

Kenji: Did you _____ it?

Salma: Yeah, the food was _____ good, but it was _____ _____. I couldn't _____ it all.

Yolanda: Salma was _____ when I took the _____ home in a doggie bag.

Kenji: Yeah, that's funny, _____ it? They call it a _____ bag, but it's for people. Anyway, what _____ surprised you?

Salma: That the restaurant was so _____! We don't use

_____ conditioning so much in my country. Oh, and the

water had _____ in it, too. I had to put on my

_____, I was so cold!

Now read the conversation with two other classmates. Practice stressing words correctly.

Reductions

6 Comparing Reduced and Unreduced Pronunciation The following sentences come from the conversation. Listen for the difference between unreduced and reduced pronunciation. Repeat both forms after the speaker.

Unreduced Pronunciation	Reduced Pronunciation*
1. Is this your first trip to the United States?	Is thishyer first trip to the United States?
2. What's your impression so far?	Whatcher impression so far?
3. I wanted her to try something exotic.	I wanted 'er ta try something exotic.

7 Listening for Reductions Anita and Brenda have just finished eating lunch together. Listen to their conversation. Repeat each sentence during the pause. Then write the unreduced forms of the missing words in the blanks.

Anita: Well, it's time to get back to the office. I'll see you soon, Brenda.

Brenda: OK, see you . . . Wait, Anita, is _____ _____ cell phone?

Anita: Oh my goodness, yes, thanks. By the way, I almost forgot: my parents are coming _____ a visit next week.

Brenda: Really? I'd love _____ meet _____.

Anita: Well, _____ _____ _____ _____ have lunch with us on Saturday?

Brenda: Saturday? Hmm . . . I promised my roommate I would go shopping with _____ that day. Could we get together _____ coffee later in the afternoon?

Anita: I _____ _____. They might be busy, but I'll ask.

With a partner, read the conversation. Practice reduced pronunciation.

---

* Note: The underlined forms are not acceptable spellings in written English.

After You Listen

8 **Using Vocabulary** Discuss the following questions with a partner. Use the underlined vocabulary in your answers.

1. Do you remember the first time you visited a foreign country? What was your first <u>impression</u> of it?

2. Has anything changed in your life in the past year? For example, did you start a new job? Did you move to a new place? Are you <u>used to</u> the new situation in your life?

3. What is the most <u>exotic</u> place or food that you have experienced in your life?

4. What would happen if an American asked for a <u>doggie bag</u> in your country?

5. How many years of education have you completed <u>so far</u>?

6. What <u>amazes</u> you about the United States or another country you have visited?

   Finish this sentence: "I am <u>amazed</u> that. . . ."

7. Some people hate to eat <u>leftovers</u>. How about you?

Talk It Over

9 **Discussing Behavior** In this section you learned the expression "When in Rome, do as the Romans do." But is this always a good rule to follow? Work in small groups and discuss the following questions.

1. Have you ever been in a situation where everyone was behaving in a way that you didn't like? How did you feel? What did you do?

2. In what situations might it be impossible for you to "do as the Romans do"? Brainstorm a list of situations. What would you do if you found yourself in one of these situations?

Before You Listen

1 Prelistening Questions Before you listen, talk with a partner about coming of age in different countries.

1. At what age does a person come of age, or become a legal adult, in your culture?

2. Do you know of any special customs or ceremonies when a person becomes an adult? Is it different for boys and girls?

▲ These young women celebrate Coming-of-Age Day in Japan.

2 Previewing Vocabulary You will hear the following words in the lecture. Listen to the words. Then write the letter of the correct definition beside each word.

Words

1. _____ the woods
2. _____ adult
3. _____ adulthood
4. _____ ceremony
5. _____ responsible for (something)
6. _____ passage
7. _____ look forward to (something)

Definitions

a. a formal or traditional way of celebrating an important event

b. the time of life when a person is not a child anymore

c. to wait for an event with a feeling of pleasure

d. a movement to the next stage or level of something

e. an area thickly covered with trees

f. in control of something and taking care of it

g. a person who is grown up, not a child anymore

Listen

3 Listening for Main Ideas Listen to a short lecture about becoming an adult in four different cultures. As you listen, list the cultures in the spaces below.

1. _____

2. _____

3. _____

4. _____

223

 4 **Taking Notes on Specific Information** Listen again. This time, fill in the details about each culture or religion.

Culture / Religion	Age	Details
1. North American Indian	12–13	
2.		
3.		
4.		

After You Listen

 5 **Summarizing Ideas** In groups of four, use your notes from Activities 3 and 4 to summarize the lecture. Each student should speak about one culture. Try to speak in complete sentences.

 6 **Using Vocabulary** Discuss the following questions with a partner. Use the underlined vocabulary in your answers.

   1. Are you legally an <u>adult</u>?

   2. Which is easier, in your opinion: <u>adulthood</u> or childhood? Why?

   3. In your community, is there a <u>ceremony</u> when a baby is born? If yes, describe it.

   4. When you were a teenager, were you <u>responsible for</u> watching your younger brothers and sisters? How did you feel about this responsibility?

5. What has been the most important <u>passage</u> in your <u>life</u> until now?

6. Are you <u>looking forward to</u> the next passage in your life (graduation, marriage, children, retirement, etc.)? Why or why not?

7. How would you feel about going into <u>the woods</u> alone for three days? Why would you feel this way?

Talk It Over

7 **At What Age . . . ?** Work in small groups. Talk about when people should be allowed to do the following activities.

Examples

I think 16 is too young to get a driver's license. Age 18 is better because . . .

▲ A teenage driver

Activity	Age
get a driver's license	
get married with parents' permission	
get married without parents' permission	
vote	
get a credit card	
live away from parents	
join the army	
become president of your country	
retire (with full government benefits)	

Getting Meaning from Context

Strategy

Graphic Organizer: Matrix Diagram

A matrix diagram organizes information about two or more characteristics of two or more topics. You can use a matrix diagram to:

- show the characteristics clearly
- study and remember the characteristics
- compare the characteristics
- organize your ideas about the characteristics

1 Prelistening Discussion When you visit other countries, it's important to know the local customs. Polite behavior in one culture can be rude in another culture. For example, kissing a friend to say hello is normal in France but not in Korea. Give examples of some polite and rude behaviors from your culture. Discuss with your group and fill in the chart.

Polite Behaviors	Rude Behaviors
being on time for appointments	being late for an appointment and not calling

Focus on Testing

Using Context Clues Many tests such as the TOEFL® iBT measure your academic listening and speaking abilities. This activity, and others in the book, will develop your social and academic communication abilities, and provide a foundation for success on a variety of standardized tests. The following five conversations take place in North America. In each situation, one speaker's action is "culturally incorrect." Listen and decide what the mistake is.

1. Listen to the beginning of each conversation.

2. Listen to the question for each conversation. Stop the recording and choose the best answer to each question.

3. In the **Clues** column, write the words that helped you choose your answer.

4. Start the recording again. Listen to the last part of each conversation to hear the correct answer.

Answers	Clues
1. (A) She didn't call before visiting. (B) She didn't bring a present. (C) She used Belinda's first name.	
2. (A) He didn't eat all his food. (B) He forgot to leave a tip. (C) He asked for the check.	
3. (A) The guests did because they were late. (B) The neighbor did because she wasn't ready. (C) The man did because he came too early.	
4. (A) He asked about the price of the house. (B) He asked too many questions. (C) He asked the woman for a drink.	
5. (A) that Koreans hug people on their birthdays (B) that Koreans don't celebrate birthdays (C) that Koreans don't hug people they don't know very well	

Talk It Over

2 Comparing Customs Review the mistakes you heard in the Focus on Testing Activity. With a partner, make a statement about each custom. Then compare it to customs in other countries.

1. In American restaurants, a 15 to 20 percent tip is normal. But in _____
_____

2. Before visiting someone in the United States, it's better to call first. But in
_____

3. _____
_____

4. _____
_____

5. _____
_____

Using Language Functions

APOLOGIZING

The following expressions are often used after we make a mistake and feel bad about a situation. The mistake may be small (stepping on someone's foot) or serious (being a half hour late for a test).

	Apologizing	**Responding**
Informal	Oops! Excuse me.	Forget about it.
↓	Sorry.	Don't worry about it.
	I'm (very) sorry.	No problem.
	It was my fault.	That's okay.
	I apologize.	That's all right.
Formal	Please forgive me.	I forgive you.

3 **Role-Play** Read the following situations. With a partner, prepare a conversation about each situation. Use the appropriate expressions for apologizing and responding.

▲ It's 6 o'clock in the morning on a Saturday.

Situations

1. It's 6 o'clock in the morning on a Saturday. Your neighbor comes to your door to complain that your music is too loud.

2. You forgot about your doctor's appointment at 3:00 P.M. today. The doctor's secretary calls you to ask what happened.

3. You don't feel well and you need to leave in the middle of the class.

4. You see an old friend and she looks like she has gained weight. You think she is pregnant. You ask her when the baby is due. She says she is not pregnant.

▲ A formal dinner party in the United States.

Culture Note

Formal Dining

Family dinners in the United States are usually relaxed and informal. However, sometimes, when special guests are invited, or if you are eating in a restaurant, dinners are more formal and traditional.

A formal American dinner usually has the following parts, served in order:

1. soup
2. salad
3. the *main course* (meat, chicken, or fish; potato or rice; and one or more cooked vegetables)
4. dessert (something sweet such as cake, ice cream, or fruit)

Typically, bread and butter are served before the salad is served. Water is almost always served.

While you are waiting for your meal, sometimes an appetizer (a small dish) will be served.

1 Prelistening Questions Before you listen, talk about dining customs with a partner.

1. What are the typical parts of a formal dinner in your culture?

2. What special foods or drinks are served at formal dinners that you don't usually have every day?

4. Have you ever eaten in a formal restaurant or at a formal dinner party? Describe this experience.

2 Previewing Vocabulary Listen to the underlined words. You will hear these words in the conversation. Before you listen, use the context to guess their definitions. Write the letter of the correct definition beside each sentence.

Sentences

1. _____ Take a couple of napkins. These sandwiches are really messy.

2. _____ When I was a teenager, it was my job to set the table each night before dinner.

3. _____ In a restaurant, it is a waiter's job to serve the food and drinks.

4. _____ Please lay that box on the dining room table.

5. _____ Europeans use silverware to eat with, while many Asians prefer chopsticks.

6. _____ Be careful with that knife! Pick it up only by the handle.

7. _____ A: What kind of kitchen utensil is this? B: It's a potato peeler. It's much easier to use than a knife.

8. _____ It is logical not to eat food that tastes bad.

Definitions

a. any kind of kitchen tool

b. knives, forks, and spoons

c. the part of a tool that you hold in your hand

d. to put dishes, plates, glasses, etc. on a table before a meal

e. reasonable or sensible

f. put something down

g. to give or bring something to a customer

h. a piece of cloth or paper used to protect your clothes and wipe your mouth while eating

3 Following Directions for Setting a Table Ming loves cooking and entertaining. For Peter's 23rd birthday, she wants to prepare a formal dinner for their friends. She asks Peter's mother, Mrs. Riley, to teach her how to set a formal dinner table.

Listen to the conversation between Ming and Mrs. Riley. Follow Mrs. Riley's instructions for setting the table. As she mentions each item, write its number in the proper place.

1. dinner napkin
2. water glass
3. white wine glass
4. red wine glass
5. bread plate
6. soup spoon
7. dessert spoon
8. dinner fork
9. salad fork
10. dessert fork
11. butter knife
12. dinner knife

4 Using Vocabulary With a partner, look at the picture from Activity 3. Take turns naming the numbered items and saying where they belong. Begin like this: "Number 1 is a napkin. It goes on the dinner plate." Then answer the questions below.

1. In your family, who <u>serves</u> the food when you eat together? Who <u>sets</u> the table?

2. What is your favorite or most useful kitchen <u>utensil</u>?

3. When you come home from school, where do you <u>lay</u> your books?

4. Do you think it is more <u>logical</u> to eat dessert before or after a meal? Why?

5. Name several utensils that have <u>handles</u>.

5 Talking About Table Manners "Table manners" means polite behavior while eating. The picture below contains ten examples of behaviors that are rude in the United States. Work in small groups. Identify the rude behaviors. Write your answers on a separate piece of paper.

<table>
<tr><td>

Culture Note

People from most countries think that Americans are very informal. For example, Americans wear jeans to restaurants, they eat while they're walking down the street, and they use people's first names in almost every situation.

However, in some situations, Americans are very formal. They follow rules of polite social behavior called etiquette. These rules tell people how to dress, talk, eat, and much more.

</td></tr>
</table>

Answer the question about manners with your group.

Which of these behaviors would be bad manners in other cultures? Which would not? What are some other eating behaviors that are rude in other cultures?

Self-Assessment Log

Check the words you learned in this chapter.

Nouns
- ❑ adult
- ❑ adulthood
- ❑ ceremony
- ❑ doggie bag
- ❑ handle
- ❑ impression
- ❑ leftovers
- ❑ napkin
- ❑ passage
- ❑ patio
- ❑ silverware
- ❑ utensil
- ❑ the woods

Verbs
- ❑ lay
- ❑ look forward to (something)
- ❑ serve
- ❑ set the table

Adjectives
- ❑ amazed
- ❑ exotic
- ❑ logical
- ❑ responsible for (something)

Expressions
- ❑ so far
- ❑ used to

Check the things you did in this chapter. How well can you do each one?

	Very well	Fairly well	Not very well
I can listen to and practice stress and reductions.	❑	❑	❑
I can talk about cultural differences.	❑	❑	❑
I can take notes on a lecture.	❑	❑	❑
I can summarize my notes.	❑	❑	❑
I can guess meanings from context.	❑	❑	❑
I can make and respond to apologies.	❑	❑	❑
I can talk about dining customs and table manners.	❑	❑	❑

Write what you learned and liked in this chapter.

In this chapter,

I learned _____

_____

I liked _____

_____

7

Health

In This Chapter

Conversation:	Touring a Health Club
Presentation:	Treating an Illness
Getting Meaning from Context:	Talking About Health
Real-World Tasks:	Talking to Health Care Professionals

❝ Laughter is the best medicine. ❞

—Proverb

Connecting to the Topic

1. Who do you see in the photo? What are they doing?

2. What are three things a person can do to stay healthy?

3. What are the most popular forms of exercise in your country? Why do you think they are so popular?

Before You Listen

1 **Prelistening Questions** Before you listen, talk about your health with a partner.

1. Do you belong to a gym or health club? How often do you go?

2. What kinds of classes and activities do health clubs offer?

3. What activities do you do to try to stay healthy?

4. Do you have any habits that are bad for your health?

▲ Kenji and Peter at the gym

2 **Previewing Vocabulary** Listen to these words and phrases from the conversation. Then complete the sentences with the words and phrases.

Nouns	Verbs	Expression
boxing	lift weights	in good/bad shape
cardio	jog	
discount	ought to	
health club	show (someone)	
lane	around	
locker room	swim	
yoga		

1. The new _____ will be very popular because it has a huge swimming pool, a great weight room, lots of exercise equipment, and a cool juice bar.

2. Some people _____ at health clubs to build stronger and bigger muscles.

3. Judy goes to the gym three times a week because she wants to be

   _____. She likes to look and feel healthy.

4. The swimming pool at my gym is separated into three sections. Fast swimmers

   swim in the middle _____ and slow swimmers swim in the other two.

5. Right now there is a 15 percent _____ on all running shoes. I got a $100.00 pair of shoes for $85.00.

6. If you want to take a _____ class, you need to buy special gloves and shoes. You need something to protect your teeth, too, in case you get hit in the mouth.

7. She likes to _____ five miles every morning before breakfast. She has to buy new running shoes every six months.

8. If you want to lose weight, you _____ eat less and exercise more.

9. If you'd like to see all of the different rooms that our health club has, I can

   _____ you _____.

10. _____ helps me to relax and stretch my muscles.

11. I love my _____ class because our teacher always chooses great, fast music for exercising. The music is so energizing that it's easy to jump around for an hour.

12. You can leave your clothes in the _____ when you go out to

    _____ in the pool.

Listen

3 **Listening for Main Ideas** Peter and Kenji want to get in shape. Close your book as you listen to the conversation. Listen for the answers to these questions.

1. Where are Peter and Kenji? How well do you think they like this place? How do you know?

2. What is the purpose of the tour? What would the guide like Peter and Kenji to do?

Compare and discuss your answers with a partner.

4 **Listening for Details** Listen again if necessary. Answer the questions.

1. What kind of exercise class did Peter and Kenji see?

2. What other classes does this gym offer?

3. Who was the fast swimmer in the pool?

4. Why should Peter and Kenji join the club this month?

Stress

5 **Listening for Stressed Words** Listen to the conversation again. Some of the stressed words are missing. During each pause, repeat the phrase or sentence. Then fill in the blanks with the words you hear.

Adel: Hi, I'm Adel. I'm _____ you're going to

_____ it here. Let me show you _____.

Here's the _____ room. We've got the newest machines,

our instructors can _____ you how to

_____ them.

Peter: This is _____!

Kenji: Yeah. I really need to start _____ _____.

Adel: And here is a _____ class . . .

Peter: I've _____ tried cardio. It's just _____, isn't it?

Adel: Not really. Actually, they're working _____ than you

_____.

Kenji: And cardio is very good for your _____.

Adel: It sure is. But you should do it at least _____ times a

week if you want to be in _____ _____.

Peter: Well, I already _____ three times a week.

Adel: That's _____.

Kenji: You also have _____ and _____ classes

here, _____ you?

Adel: Yes. I'll give you a _____ of classes when we finish our

_____. Now here's our _____ pool.

Peter: Wow! Look at that woman in the _____ lane. She's really

fast, _____ she!

Adel: Oh, yeah. That's Ellen, one of our _____.

Kenji: _____ like to take lessons from _____!

Adel: You're not the _____ one. C'mon, I'll show you the

_____ and the locker room.

Adel: You know, if you want to _____ our gym, you

_____ to do it _____ the end of the

month.

Kenji: Really? Why?

Adel: Well, because we have a special _____ for students this

month. _____ go to my office and I'll

_____ you all about it.

Now read the conversation with two other classmates. Practice stressing words correctly.

After You Listen

 6 Using Vocabulary Discuss the following questions with a partner. Use the
underlined vocabulary in your answers.

1. Which of the following activities have you tried? Did you like or dislike them?
   Why?

   <u>lifting weights</u>   <u>jogging</u>   <u>boxing</u>   <u>yoga</u>   <u>swimming</u>

2. Are you <u>in good shape</u> now? If yes, how do you keep in shape? If not, what can
   you do to get in shape?

3. Are you a good <u>swimmer</u>? When did you learn to <u>swim</u>? How did you learn?
   If you can't swim, are you interested in learning? Why, or why not?

4. Do you think it's fair that students and senior citizens can get <u>discounts</u> at
   <u>health clubs</u>, theaters, restaurants, and other places? Why, or why not?

5. Is it safe to leave your money and other valuable things in the <u>locker room</u> at a
   gym? Why, or why not?

6. Your friend wants to get in shape quickly. Tell your friend what he or she
   <u>ought to</u> do.

Pronunciation

INTONATION WITH TAG QUESTIONS

A tag question is a statement with a "tag" at the end. Affirmative statements take negative tags, and negative statements take affirmative tags.
For example:

He's strong, isn't he?   You're not tired, are you?

People pronounce tag questions in two ways. Listen to the following examples. Notice the difference in intonation.

<table>
<tr><td>Rising Intonation</td><td>Falling Intonation</td></tr>
<tr><td>Your father is a doctor, isn't he?</td><td>Your father is a doctor, isn't he?</td></tr>
</table>

In the first example, the speaker isn't sure of the answer. He is asking for information, so his voice goes up at the end of the sentence:

Your father is a doctor, isn't he?

In the second example, the speaker is sure that the father is a doctor. The question is not a real question; instead, it is a way of "making conversation." The speaker's voice goes down at the end of the sentence:

Your father is a doctor, isn't he?

Culture Note

English speakers often use **tag questions** to start conversations with strangers in public places, for example, at a bus stop, in a supermarket line, in a doctor's waiting room, in an elevator. The tag questions are always about something general, not personal.

Examples
This elevator is really slow, **isn't it**?
This market has excellent produce, **doesn't it**?

7 Pronouncing Tag Questions Listen and repeat the sentences. The first five are asking for information, so they have rising intonation. The second five are ways of making conversation. They have falling intonation.

1. We need special shoes for cardio, don't we?

2. The pool is warm, isn't it?

3. You play football, don't you?

4. You don't eat junk food, do you?

5. You didn't hurt yourself, did you?

6. My father looks healthy, doesn't he?

7. This exercise is hard, isn't it?

8. Your parents love to dance, don't they?

9. She can swim fast, can't she?

10. It's a beautiful day, isn't it?

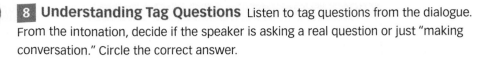

8 **Understanding Tag Questions** Listen to tag questions from the dialogue. From the intonation, decide if the speaker is asking a real question or just "making conversation." Circle the correct answer.

1. Asking a question   Making conversation
2. Asking a question   Making conversation
3. Asking a question   Making conversation
4. Asking a question   Making conversation
5. Asking a question   Making conversation
6. Asking a question   Making conversation

Using Language Functions

FORMING TAG QUESTIONS

When the verb *be* is used in the main statement of the sentence, use *be* to form the tag question. For example:

Vic **is** tired, **isn't** he?   Lori **isn't** here, **is** she?

When a modal verb (like *can, could, should, would*) is used in the main statement of the sentence, use the same verb to form the tag question. For example:

Tzu Han **can** swim, **can't** she?   Yong Jin **shouldn't** go, **should** he?

When other verbs are used in the main statement of the sentence, use *do* to form the tag question. For example:

Farida **plays** tennis, **doesn't** she?   Linda **doesn't** have a car, **does** she?

9 **Using Tag Questions** Work with a partner. Each of you will look at a different set of sentences in the box on page 128. Add a tag question to each sentence. Use rising intonation if you don't know what your partner's answer will be. Use falling intonation if you know the answer. You should both answer truthfully.*

Example (Hamburgers are fattening.)
Student A asks: Hamburgers are fattening, aren't they?
Student B answers: Yes, I think so. (means Student A is correct.)

---

* If a tag question is affirmative, answer "No" if you agree with the speaker. Answer "Yes" if you disagree. For example:
A: There's no homework tonight, is there?
B: No, there isn't. (means Speaker A is correct)
B: Yes, there is. (means Speaker A is incorrect)

Talk It Over

▲ A woman meditating

▲ Stockbrokers

10 Talking About Stress You are going to complete a questionnaire about stress. First, discuss the following questions with your classmates and teacher.

1. What is stress?

2. What causes stress?

3. What can be the results of living with too much stress?

4. When do you feel you are under a lot of stress?

11 Completing a Questionnaire About Stress Complete the following questionnaire.*

How stressful is your life? Give yourself points from one to five on each item:

1 = almost always
2 = often
3 = sometimes
4 = seldom
5 = never

1. _____ I eat at least one hot, nutritious meal a day (a meal that has all the basic foods needed for good health).

2. _____ I get seven to eight hours of sleep at least four nights a week.

3. _____ I give and receive affection regularly.

4. _____ I have at least one relative within fifty miles on whom I can rely, who could help me if I needed help.

5. _____ I exercise fairly heavily (to the point of perspiration) at least twice a week.

6. _____ I am the appropriate weight for my height.

7. _____ I have an income that is enough to meet the basic expenses.

8. _____ I get strength from my religious beliefs.

9. _____ I regularly attend club or social activities.

10. _____ I have a network, or group, of friends and acquaintances.

11. _____ I have one or more friends to talk to about personal matters.

12. _____ I am in good health (including eyesight, hearing, teeth).

13. _____ I am able to speak openly about my feelings when angry or worried.

14. _____ I have regular conversations with the people I live with about domestic problems—for example, chores, money, and daily living issues.

15. _____ I do something for fun at least once a week.

16. _____ I am able to organize my time effectively.

17. _____ I drink fewer than three cups of coffee (or tea or cola drinks) a day.

18. _____ I take quiet time for myself during the day.

---

* Questionnaire and scoring chart taken from "How Vulnerable Are You to Stress", *Time Magazine,* © Time Inc. Reprinted by permission.

To find your score, add up the numbers and subtract 20. Then check the chart below to analyze your score.

	If your score is . . . ,	you are . . .
Safe Zone	below 25	living a calm, unstressful life.
Leaving the Safe Zone	between 25 and 45	living with more stress than experts consider healthy. Maybe you should think about making some changes.
Moving Near the Danger Zone	between 45 and 70	approaching the danger zone. Which of the 20 areas can you change?
Danger Zone	over 70	living with entirely too much stress. You may have serious problems as a result.

 12 Follow-Up Discuss these questions with the whole class or in small groups.

1. Who had the highest score in the class? The lowest?

2. Look at the 18 items. Find two areas that you would like to change in your life. Tell your classmates about these two areas. Then listen as they tell you about the areas they would like to change.

Part 2 A Doctor's Advice: Treating an Illness

Before You Listen

1 Prelistening Questions. Before you listen, talk about the flu with a partner.

1. Have you ever had the flu (influenza)?

2. What are the *symptoms* of the flu? (For example: a fever)

3. Imagine that you are a doctor. What advice would you give a patient who has the flu?

Graphic Organizer: Problem-Solution Chart
You can use a problem-solution chart to list problems and possible ways to solve them. In the chart below, the problem column is Symptoms of the Flu and the solution column is Treatment of the Flu.

2 **Previewing Vocabulary** Listen to the words from the conversation. Then in a small group, divide the expressions into two groups in the graphic organizer below: "Symptoms of the Flu" and "Treatment of the Flu." Use a dictionary if necessary.

Nouns	**Adjectives**	**Expression**
aspirin	swollen	eat right
fever	weak	
headache		
prescription		
rest		
sore throat		
upset stomach		

Symptoms of the Flu	Treatment of the Flu

The following body parts are mentioned in the conversation. Define them before you listen. Work with a partner.

muscle _____

forehead _____

throat _____

Listen

 3 **Listening for Main Ideas** Barbara is at the university health service. Listen to her conversation with her doctor. As you listen, answer these questions.

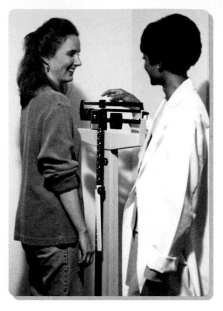

1. What is wrong with Barbara?

2. What does the doctor tell her to do?

 4 **Taking Notes on Specific Information** Listen to the conversation again. This time, take notes in the problem-solution chart below.

Barbara's Complaints	Doctor's Advice
1.	
2.	
3.	
4.	
5.	
6.	

After You Listen

5 **Summarizing Ideas** Use past-tense verbs to summarize Barbara's visit to the doctor. Include her symptoms and the doctor's advice.

Example

> Barbara went to the doctor because she woke up with a terrible headache. She told the doctor . . .

6 **Reviewing Vocabulary** Answer the questions with a classmate.

1. Look back at Activity 2 on page 131. Which symptoms did you have the last time you had the flu or a cold?

2. How often do you take pain pills such as aspirin?

3. Look back at the doctor's advice. Which advice do you agree with, or disagree with? Why?

Using Language Functions

GIVING ADVICE

Here are some expressions for asking for and giving advice.

Asking for Advice	Giving Advice
What should I do?	You should . . .
What do you think I should do?	You ought to . . .
What do you think I ought to do?	Try to . . .
Should I _____?	Why don't you . . .
Can you give me some/any advice?	I advise you to . . .

▲ "Can you give me some advice?"

7 Asking for and Giving Advice

1. Work with a partner. Describe the problem in each of the following pictures.

2. Match the picture with the correct remedy (treatment).

3. Finally, role-play each situation. One person describes the problem and asks for advice. The other person gives advice.

Example

A: I have a headache. Should I go to a doctor?

B: I don't think so. Why don't you take an aspirin?

> **Possible Remedies**
> **a.** Drink tea.   **d.** Put ice on it.
> **b.** Take a cold shower.   **e.** Take a sleeping pill.
> **c.** Bandage it.

1. ____

2. ____

3. ____

4. ____

5. ____

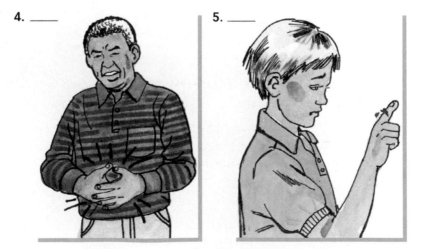

Part 3

Strategies for Better Listening and Speaking

Getting Meaning from Context

Focus on Testing

Using Context Clues

Many tests such as the TOEFL® iBT measure your academic listening and speaking abilities. This activity, and others in the book, will develop your social and communication skills, and provide a foundation for success on a variety of standardized tests. Each of the following four conversations has one surprising or unusual thing in it.

1. Listen to each conversation. Then listen to the question. Stop the recording after the question, and write what is strange in the **Answers** column in the chart.

2. In the **Clues** column, write the words that helped you choose your answer.

3. Start the recording again.

4. Listen to the next part of the conversation to hear the correct answer.

Answers	Clues
1.	
2.	
3.	
4.	

Now listen to the following conversations. What are they about? Choose the best answer to each question.

1. Ⓐ Nancy's having an operation.
   Ⓑ Nancy's going to have a baby.
   Ⓒ Nancy's working at the hospital.

2. Ⓐ coffee shop
   Ⓑ supermarket
   Ⓒ health food store

1 Role-Play People have different ways of getting help with their personal problems. Some people visit psychologists for advice, while others talk to their close friends and family members about their problems.

With a partner, prepare a role-play taking the roles of a friend or family member and someone with one of the problems in the box below.

> You are very shy at parties and at work.
>
> You cannot stay with just one girlfriend/boyfriend.
>
> You are jealous of your very successful sister.
>
> You work 18 hours a day and don't know how to relax.

▲ Which woman is offering advice?

2 Discussing Your Opinion In small groups, read the statements about smoking. Then say if you agree or disagree with each statement, and give reasons for your opinion.

▲ You cannot smoke in this place. What kind of place do you think this is?

1. Smoking should be forbidden in:

   - restaurants
   - movie theaters
   - classrooms
   - bars

   - public transportation
   - hospitals
   - discos/nightclubs.
   - (your suggestion): _____

2. It should be illegal to sell cigarettes to anyone under the age of 18.

3. If a smoker gets cancer, it's his own fault. Nobody forced him to smoke.

4. If a smoker gets cancer, the tobacco companies should pay her medical bills.

5. It is wrong to advertise cigarettes to teenagers.

6. I would not date a person who smokes.

7. Governments should educate their people, especially teenagers, about the dangers of smoking.

8. If parents smoke, their children will probably smoke also.

9. There should not be cigarette advertising:

   - on television
   - on the radio

   - in magazines
   - on billboards

Part 4 Real-World Tasks: Talking to Health Care Professionals

 1 **Taking Notes on Phone Conversations.** You will hear three telephone conversations about health situations. Take notes on each call.

Conversation 1

Reason for call: _____

_____

Name of dentist: _____

Location: _____

Time of appointment: _____

Conversation 2

Reason for call: _____

_____

Name of patient: _____

Price of medicine: _____

Special instructions: _____

Closing time: _____

Conversation 3

First reason for call: _____

_____

Name of baby's doctor: _____

Time of baby's new appointment: _____

Second reason for call: _____

_____

Time of husband's appointment: _____

Name of husband's doctor: _____

2 Making Appointments with Doctors Choose one of the situations from this page or the next page to role-play with a partner. Look only at the box for your role. Do not look at your partner's information!

Situation 1: Dentist's office

Roles: patient and receptionist

> ### Patient's Instructions
> 1. Call the dentist's office to change your appointment. Tell the receptionist:
>   a. the time of your old appointment.
>   b. the reason for the change.
> 2. Arrange a new appointment time with the receptionist.

> ### Receptionist's Instructions
> 1. A patient will call you to change an appointment. Answer the phone politely; then listen to the patient's problem.
> 2. Arrange an appointment time with the patient.

Situation 2: Doctor's office

Roles: patient and receptionist

> ### Patient's Instructions
> 1. Call the doctor's office to make an appointment. Tell the receptionist:
>   a. your medical problem (why you're calling).
>   b. when you want to come in.
> 2. Ask where you can park.

> ### Receptionist's Instructions
> 1. A patient will call you to make an appointment. Answer the phone politely; then listen to the patient's problem.
> 2. Arrange an appointment time with the patient.

Language Tip

In Part 2 you learned some common symptoms of **the flu** or **a cold.** Here are additional expressions for reporting on a variety of symptoms.

I have a cough/a rash/a backache.
My arm hurts/aches.
My (eye) is sore/swollen/red.
I feel dizzy/ nauseated/tired/ hot/cold/ depressed.
I have no appetite/energy.

Situation 3: Doctor's office

Roles: patient and doctor

Patient's Instructions

1. You have a strange medical problem. Tell your doctor:
   a. your symptoms.
   b. when they started.
   c. how often you have them.

Doctor's Instructions

1. Listen to a patient tell you about his or her strange symptoms.

2. Ask the patient when these symptoms started and how often they happen.

3. Tell the patient that he or she has an unusual disease and give the patient instructions about how to treat the problem.

▲ "I'd like to change my appointment. Do you have anything available tomorrow?"

Self-Assessment Log

Check the words you learned in this chapter.

Nouns
- ❑ aspirin
- ❑ boxing
- ❑ cardio
- ❑ discount
- ❑ fever
- ❑ headache
- ❑ health club
- ❑ lane
- ❑ locker room
- ❑ prescription
- ❑ rest
- ❑ sore throat
- ❑ upset stomach
- ❑ yoga

Verbs
- ❑ jog
- ❑ lift weights
- ❑ ought to
- ❑ show (someone) around
- ❑ swim

Adjectives
- ❑ swollen
- ❑ weak

Expressions
- ❑ eat right
- ❑ in good/bad shape

Check the things you did in this chapter. How well can you do each one?

	Very well	Fairly well	Not very well
I can listen to and practice stress.	❑	❑	❑
I can listen to and use tag questions.	❑	❑	❑
I can talk about health and stress.	❑	❑	❑
I can take notes on a conversation.	❑	❑	❑
I can summarize my notes.	❑	❑	❑
I can guess meanings from context.	❑	❑	❑
I can ask for and give advice.	❑	❑	❑
I can practice making a doctor's appointment.	❑	❑	❑

Write what you learned and what you liked in this chapter.

In this chapter,

I learned _____

_____

I liked _____

_____

Entertainment and the Media

❝ Whoever controls the media—the images—controls the culture. ❞

—Allen Ginsberg
American Beat poet (1926–1997)

Connecting to the Topic

1 Look at the photo of a reality TV program. Who are the people in the photo? How do they feel?

2 What TV programs do you enjoy watching? Why?

3 What are some of your favorite advertisements? Why?

Before You Listen

 1 Prelistening Questions Before you listen, talk about television with a partner.

▲ Jack and Ming

1. How many hours of TV do you watch a week?

2. How many television sets do you have in your house? Where are they?

3. In your opinion, what's the best way to get the news: from television, a newspaper, or the Internet? Why?

2 Previewing Vocabulary Listen to the words and phrases from the conversation. Then complete the sentences with the words and phrases. Don't write anything on the lines on the left. You will use those lines in Activity 8.

Nouns	**Verbs**
average week	change channels
couch potato	channel surf
remote control	turn down the volume
the TV	turn on the TV
waste of time	turn the TV off

1. _____ As soon as I get home from work, I _____ because I want to know what's on the news.

2. _____ When friends come to visit, we usually _____ and just talk.

3. _____ When I don't like a TV show, I _____ and find another program.

4. _____ The commercials are very loud, so I _____ when they come on.

5. _____ I prefer to study in a quiet room, without _____ on.

6. _____ To find a good program on TV, I don't look in the newspaper. I usually just _____ until I find something interesting.

7. _____ I don't like to exercise or go out; I prefer to stay home and watch TV. I guess I am a(n) _____.

8. _____ It's easy to change channels with a _____.

9. _____ I think TV is very entertaining and educational, but other people think it's a(n) _____.

10. _____ I watch 20 hours of TV during a(n) _____.

Listen

3 Listening for Main Ideas Ming is visiting Jack. They are talking about television. Close your book as you listen to the conversation. Listen for the answers to these questions.

1. What do Jack and Ming think about watching TV? Do they agree or disagree?

2. Why does Ming prefer to get the news from the Internet or the newspaper?

3. What is Jack's habit when watching TV?

Compare and discuss your answers with a partner.

4 Listening for Details Listen again if necessary. Write *T* if a statement is true and *F* if it is false.

_____ **1.** The average American watches five hours of TV a day.

_____ **2.** Ming is reading a newspaper.

_____ **3.** Ming is a couch potato.

_____ **4.** Jack doesn't like soap operas.

_____ **5.** Ming and Jack don't like TV commercials.

Stress

5 Listening for Stressed Words Listen to the conversation again. Some of the stressed words are missing. During each pause, repeat the phrase or sentence. Then fill in the blanks with the words you hear.

Ming: Hey, _____ to this. The _____ American watches _____ hours of TV a day.

Jack: A day? You're _____.

Ming: No, it says so right here in this _____. Hmm, I guess _____ an average American, Jack. You _____ have your _____ on.

Jack: Come on. Are you saying I'm a _____ potato?

Ming: Yeah. I really think watching TV is a _____ of time.

Jack: Oh, come _____. _____ programs are bad, like those _____ operas. But what about sports or the _____? You watch those sometimes, don't you?

Ming: Well, actually, for the _____, I prefer the _____. Or the _____.

Jack: Why?

Ming: First, because they give you a lot more _____. And I can _____ them any time I want. Plus, I _____ all the commercials.

Jack: I know what you _____. That's why, when the commercials come on, I just _____ down the volume or change _____.

Ming: Yeah, I noticed that. Channel surfing drives me _____.

Jack: Okay, next time you come _____, I'll let you have the remote _____.

Ming: Oh, that's so sweet. But I have a _____ idea. Next time I come over, let's just turn the TV _____.

Now read the conversation with a partner. Practice stressing words correctly.

Reductions

 6 Comparing Unreduced and Reduced Pronunciation. The following sentences come from the conversation. Listen for the difference between unreduced and reduced pronunciation. Repeat both forms after the speaker.

Unreduced Pronunciation	**Reduced Pronunciation***
1. Are you saying I'm a couch potato?	<u>Arya</u> saying I'm a couch potato?
2. You watch those sometimes, don't you?	You watch those sometimes, <u>dontcha</u>?
3. I know what you mean.	I know <u>whatcha</u> mean.
4. I'll let you have the remote control.	I'll <u>letcha</u> have the remote control.

7 Listening for Reductions Listen to the following sentences. You'll hear the reduced pronunciation of some words. Repeat each sentence during the pause. Then write the unreduced forms of the missing words in the blanks.

A: _____ _____ calling the movie theater?

B: Uh-huh. _____ _____ _____
_____ go to the movies tonight?

A: To tell _____ the truth, I'm pretty tired. But we
_____ go to an early show. _____
_____ know _____ _____
_____ _____ see?

B: Not really. I'll _____ _____ choose. *Batman III* is playing at eight and James Bond is at ten.

A: Let's see *Batman III*. I'm tired now and by ten o'clock I'm _____
_____ be dead.

With a partner, read the conversation. Practice the reduced pronunciation.

_____

* Note: The underlined forms are not acceptable spellings in written English.

8 **Using Vocabulary** Look at the ten statements in Activity 2 on page 145. Check [✓] the sentences that are true for you. With a partner, discuss the sentences that are *not* true for you. Use the new vocabulary in your discussion.

Example

> Number 6 is not true in my case. I don't like to channel surf. Before I turn on the TV, I always choose a program from the TV guide. But my brother channel surfs all the time.

"Would you please pick something and quit channel surfing."

Drawing by Frascino; © 1979. The New Yorker Magzine. Inc.
The New Yorker Collection 1994 Leo Cullum from cartoonbank.com. All Rights Reserved.
Reprinted by permission.

Using Language Functions

EXPRESSING OPINIONS, AGREEING, AND DISAGREEING

When Ming and Jack had different opinions about television, they used the following language:

Ming: I really think watching TV is a waste of time.
Jack: Oh, come on!

Look at other expressions English speakers use to express opinions, to agree, and to disagree.

Expressing an Opinion

I think (that) . . .
I feel . . .
I believe . . .
In my opinion . . .

Agreeing

That's my opinion, too.
I agree (with you).
I feel the same way.
You're right.
That's a good point.

You're Not Sure

I don't have a strong opinion about that. I think it depends (on something).

Disagreeing

I disagree (with you).
I don't agree.
I don't feel the same way.
Oh, come on!*

---

* "Oh, come on!" is very informal.

9 Expressing Opinions Work in groups of three. Look at the nine t
Take turns giving your opinion on each topic like this:

> *Student A:* Give your opinion about the topic. Give reasons.
>
> *Student B:* Agree or disagree. Give reasons.
>
> *Student C:* Agree or disagree with A or B. Give reasons.

Example

Ming: I think watching TV is a waste of time. Most programs are stupid or boring.

Jack: I disagree with you. Many programs are useful—if you choose them carefully.

Peter: I agree with Ming. There are so many better things to do than sit and watch TV.

1. violence on television

2. cigarette advertisements in magazines

3. magazine stories about private lives of famous people

4. high salaries of superstar athletes

5. high salaries of movie stars

6. low salaries of teachers

7. government control of television programs (censorship)

8. high price of rock concert tickets

9. (choose your own topic)

Part 2 News Report: An Airplane Crash

Before You Listen

Strategy

Graphic Organizer: Four (Five) W's

To take notes on an event, use a four (or five) W's graphic organizer. Write questions about the situation asking *what, where, when, who,* (and possibly *why*). The answers to these four (or five) questions will give you a complete picture of the event.

1 **Prelistening Questions** Before you listen, talk about accidents with a partner.

1. Have you ever seen an accident? Describe what happened.

2. Imagine a news report about an airplane crash. Write four questions about it in the Four W's Graphic Organizer:

p. 124 (2)

	Question	
What		?
Where		?
When		?
Who		?

2 **Previewing Vocabulary** Listen to the underlined words from the conversation. You will hear the underlined words in a news report. Then, write the letter of the correct definition beside each sentence.

(Note: Two of the words have very similar meanings!)

Sentences

1. _____ What was the top story on the evening news last night?

2. _____ The airplane left Chicago at 3:00 and landed in San Francisco at 8:00.

3. _____ My sports car is so small, I can only take one passenger.

4. _____ He had two serious injuries: a broken arm and a broken knee.

5. _____ She had to go to the hospital because she was hurt in the accident.

6. _____ Dina's car broke down on the highway and blocked traffic for an hour.

7. _____ I ran out of money, so I asked my parents for $100.

Definitions

a. person in the car other than the driver

b. had no more

c. stopped something from moving

d. places where the body is damaged

e. the first story in a news program

f. experienced pain or damage to the body

g. arrived; touched the ground

Listen

3 **Listening for Main Ideas** Listen to a news report about an airplane crash.

▲ A news report about an airplane crash.

1. As you listen, write the key words in the space provided.

_____

_____

_____

_____

2. Which of the following is the main idea of the story?
  a. An airplane crashed onto the highway and everyone died.
  b. Two people saw the airplane crash and called the police.
  c. An airplane landed on the highway.

4 **Listening for Specific Information** Listen again. This time, take notes about the following details.

1. Location of the plane: _____

2. Number of passengers: _____

3. Number of passengers injured: _____

4. Type of injuries: _____

_____

5. Number of people injured on the ground: _____

6. Possible cause of crash: _____

_____

5 **Summarizing Ideas** Compare notes with a partner. Together, summarize the news report in your own words. As you speak, use your questions from Activity 1 and your notes from Activities 3 and 4 to help you remember.

6 **Using Vocabulary** Discuss the following questions with a partner. Use the underlined vocabulary in your answers.

1. Did you watch the news on TV last night? What was the top story?
2. If an airplane can't land because of bad weather, what can the pilot do?
3. On a long car trip, do you prefer to be the passenger or the driver? Why?
4. Tell about some injuries you had when you were a child. Were you hurt while playing or while doing sports? Were you seriously hurt?
5. If you run out of money while on vacation, what can you do?
6. How do you feel when someone blocks traffic unnecessarily?

Talk It Over

7 **Summarizing News Reports** Watch a news program the day before your class. Choose one of the reports in the news. Give the class a short summary of the report. Use simple words and focus on the key ideas only. Make a Five W's graphic organizer. Write questions and answers in it and use it during your presentation.

	Question	Answer
What	?	
Where	?	
When	?	
Who	?	
Why	?	

Getting Meaning from Context

TOEFL® iBT

Focus on Testing

Using Context Clues Many tests such as the TOEFL® iBT measure your academic listening and speaking abilities. This activity, and others in the book, will develop your social and academic communication abilities, and provide a foundation for success on a variety of standardized tests. You will hear five commercials. Decide which product or service they advertise.

1. Listen to the beginning of each commercial. Then listen to the question.
2. Stop the recording after each question and choose the product or service advertised.
3. In the **Clues** column, write the words that helped you choose your answer.
4. Listen to the last part of the commercial to hear the correct answer.

Answers	Clues
1. (A) soup (B) breakfast cereal (C) vitamins	
2. (A) long distance calling plan (B) sleeping pill (C) cell phone company	
3. (A) baby products (B) a used car (C) a new car	
4. (A) breakfast food (B) TV magazine (C) sleeping pill	
5. (A) comedy show (B) daytime TV drama (C) TV news program	

Talk It Over

1 **Discussing Advertisements** In small groups, discuss the qualities of a good advertisement. Make a list.

1. *It should be easy to notice.*
2. *It should be funny, so we pay attention and remember it.*
3. _____
4. _____
5. _____

Look at the following advertisement. Does it have all the qualities you just listed? Discuss what you like and don't like about this ad.

▲ An advertisement on a billboard.

Bring examples of an interesting and a boring ad from a magazine or newspaper. Explain to your classmates why you chose these ads.

1 **Types of TV Programs** Look at the types of television programs below. Give an example of each.

Types of Shows	Examples
a. reality show	*Survivor*
b. cartoon	
c. game show	
d. drama series	
e. sitcom (situation comedy)	
f. children's program	
g. news program	
h. soap opera	

Look at the list of popular TV shows from the United States and England. Match them with the types of shows above. Write the letters on lines. If you don't know some of the shows, find information on the Internet. What other popular shows do you know? Write them in the chart.

1. __g__ *CNN® International*

2. _____ *CSI*

3. _____ *Teletubbies*

4. _____ *Desperate Housewives*

5. _____ *Who Wants to Be a Millionaire?*

6. _____ *The Simpsons*

7. _____ *Big Brother*

2 **Discussing a Program Guide** Jennifer and her brother want to watch TV tonight. Before you listen, look at the TV guide on page 157 and answer these questions:

1. What's on Channel 2 at 7:00?

2. What time is the news on? What channels is it on?

3. Who will be the guests on the Oprah Winfrey show?

Now listen to the conversation. During each pause, fill in the missing information and circle the type of program. Compare your answers with classmates.

PRIME TIME MONDAY						
Channel	7:00 PM	7:30 PM	8:00 PM	8:30 PM	9:00 PM	9:30 PM
2 KCBS	**Survivor** Reality show		**America's Next Top Model** Reality show		**39th Annual Country Music Awards** Award show	
4 NBC	**Extra!** Entertainment news magazine		**The Apprentice** Reality show		**Law and Order** Crime drama	
7 KABC	_____ *(name of program)* Game show/news/cartoon		**The Oprah Winfrey Show** Special guests: celebrity couples Talk show		**News**	
11 KTTV	**Home Improvement** Comedy	**Home Improvement** Comedy	_____ *(name of program)* Soap opera/talk show/movie			
13 KCOP	**The Simpsons** Comedy	**King of the Hill** Comedy	_____ *(name of program)* Movie/news/cartoon			
20 TLC	**Alias** Crime drama		_____ *(name of program)* Horror movie/drama series/soap opera			
CNN	**Asia Today** News show		**Live from Washington** News show	**News**	**Larry King Live** Talk show	
25 ESPN	**NFL Live** Sports		**Sports Center** Sports news		_____ *(name of program)* Documentary/talk show/sports	
53 FX	**That 70's Show** Comedy		_____ *(name of program)* Cartoon/children's show/sitcom	**Seinfeld**	**Mission Impossible** Action adventure	**Fear Factor** Reality show

page 11

3 **Describing a Favorite Show or Movie** Tell a partner about your favorite TV show or movie. To help you organize your description, make notes about the points listed below.

1. Kind of show (drama, talk show, comedy, etc.):

_____

2. Type of people in it (young, single people; married couple; etc.):

_____

3. Situation (city police station, apartment building, etc.):

_____

4. Reasons you like it (funny characters, exciting story, educational, etc.):

_____

Example

I like to watch *Desperate Housewives.* It's a kind of soap opera about four housewives. They live in a very nice neighborhood and have different types of families and personalities. Each episode tells some secret about the housewives and their neighbors. I like the show because sometimes it's funny and other times it's very dramatic. I watch it every week to see what happens to the characters and how the housewives solve their problems.

▲ A scene from *Desperate Housewives,* an American TV show.

Self-Assessment Log

Check the words you learned in this chapter.

Nouns

- ❑ average week
- ❑ couch potato
- ❑ injury
- ❑ passenger
- ❑ remote control
- ❑ run out of
- ❑ top story
- ❑ the TV
- ❑ waste of time

Verbs

- ❑ block
- ❑ change channels
- ❑ channel surf
- ❑ hurt
- ❑ land
- ❑ turn down the volume
- ❑ turn on the TV
- ❑ turn the TV off

Check the things you did in this chapter. How well can you do each one?

	Very well	Fairly well	Not very well
I can listen to and practice stress and reductions.	❑	❑	❑
I can express my opinions.	❑	❑	❑
I can take notes on a news report.	❑	❑	❑
I can summarize my notes.	❑	❑	❑
I can guess meanings from context.	❑	❑	❑
I can talk about TV shows and advertisements.	❑	❑	❑

Write what you learned and what you liked in this chapter.

In this chapter,

I learned _____

_____

I liked _____

_____

Social Life

In This Chapter

❝ A friend to all is a friend to none. ❞

—Greek proverb

1. Look at the photo. Where are these people? What are they doing?

2. What types of activities do you like to do with your friends?

3. What are the qualities of a good friend?

Before You Listen

 1 Prelistening Questions Talk about your oldest friends with a partner.

▲ Ming and Yolanda run into Dan.

1. Look at the photo. Have Ming and Yolanda seen Dan recently? Did they expect to see him?

2. How long have you known your closest friends? Since elementary school? Middle school? High school? College? After college?

3. Have you ever had a *reunion* with old friends? What did you talk about? Did you stay in touch after that?

4. Have you ever run into an old friend by accident? Where and when?

2 Previewing Vocabulary Listen to these words and expressions from the conversation. Complete the sentences below the chart with the words and expressions. Then write the examples and the meanings of the expressions in the chart.

Words and Expressions	Use of Words and Expressions in the Sentences	Meanings As Used Here
good at	"He has always been good at science."	He's able to understand science easily.
graduation		
keep in touch		
make sense		
on the road		
pre-med		
sales rep		
terrific		
be up to		

1. Dan plans to become a doctor because he has always been

    _____ science.

2. **Ming:** Hi, Dan. I haven't seen you in a while. What have you been

    _____ ?

    Dan: Not much. Just studying and going to school.

3. I love your new haircut. It really looks _____ .

4. I'm _____ most of the time because my company needs me to travel a lot.

5. Yolanda wants to go to medical school after college, so she's studying

    _____ courses in college now.

6. I send email to my friends every week because I want to _____ with them.

7. To celebrate my _____ from high school, my parents bought me a new computer. It will be great to have a new computer when I go to college in the fall.

8. It doesn't _____ to buy a car if you live five minutes from your university.

9. **Yolanda:** I took this job because I am really good at selling things!

   Dan: Oh! So you're a _____?

Listen

3 Listening for Main Ideas Dan is visiting his hometown. He runs into two of his high school classmates walking down the street. Close your book as you listen. Prepare to answer these questions.

1. What is the main thing the three friends discuss?

2. Dan says he's been studying hard. What do the women think?

3. At the end of the conversation, what do the friends say they will do?

Compare and discuss your answers with a partner.

4 Listening for Details Listen again if necessary. Answer these questions.

1. When was the last time Dan saw Yolanda and Ming?

2. What is Dan's major?

3. Ming is a sales rep. Where does Yolanda work?

Stress

5 Listening for Stressed Words Listen to the conversation again. Some of the stressed words are missing. During each pause, repeat the phrase or sentence. Then fill in the blanks with words you hear.

Yolanda: Ming, look! I can't __believe__ it! It's Dan. Hey Dan! How are you?

Dan: Yolanda? Ming? Wow! I haven't seen you guys since __grad-__ night!

Ming: I know. You look __great__!

Dan: Thanks. So do __you__!

Ming: So what have you been __up__ to?

Dan: Well, I go to Faber College.

Yolanda: __Really__? Do you __like__ it?

Dan: Yeah, _____so_____ _____far_____. But I've been _____studying_____ really hard.

Ming: _____Sure_____ you have . . .

Yolanda: So, what's your major?

Dan: It's _____computer_____ science.

Ming: Ah-h-h. _____that_____ makes sense. You always _____were_____ good at _____math_____ and _____science_____.

Dan: Thanks. Anyway, what have _____you_____ guys been up to?

Ming: Well, I'm a _____sales_____ rep for a publishing company.

Dan: No _____kidding_____! How do you like that?

Ming: Oh, I _____love_____ it! I'm on the road a lot, but I get to meet some interesting people.

Dan: That's _____terrific_____. And how about _____you_____, Yolanda?

Yolanda: I'm studying _____Pre-med_____ at State College.

Dan: Wow—you can be my doctor! You always were _____good_____ at science too. Well, it was great seeing you both. Let's keep in _____touch_____ from now on. Email me sometime. Here's my address.

Now read the conversation with two classmates. Practice stressing words correctly.

After You Listen

6 **Using Vocabulary** Discuss the following questions with a partner. Use the underlined vocabulary in your answers.

1. What have you <u>been up to</u> (during the past year)—besides studying English?

2. Tell about a restaurant that is a <u>terrific</u> place to go on a date, in your opinion. Why is it so great?

3. Tell about something your friends or family might think you are <u>good at</u>.

4. Do you <u>keep in touch</u> with any of your friends or teachers from when you were younger? Who?

5. Would you like a job that required you to be <u>on the road</u> 50 percent of the time?

6. Give several reasons why it <u>makes sense</u> or doesn't <u>make sense</u> for students to wear uniforms in school.

Pronunciation

To express strong feelings (surprise, anger, happiness), we use exclamations. These are expressions that we pronounce with especially strong emphasis and with falling intonation at the end.

Examples

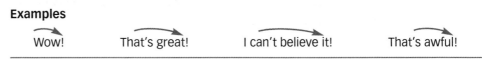

Wow!   That's great!   I can't believe it!   That's awful!

7 Pronouncing Exclamations Repeat the following exclamations from the conversation. Follow the stress and intonation patterns carefully.

1. Ming, look!
2. I can't believe it!
3. Wow! I haven't seen you guys since graduation night!
4. You look great!
5. So do you!
6. No kidding!
7. That's terrific!

8 **Matching Statements and Responses** Listen to these eight statements or questions. Choose the appropriate responses from the box and write their letters in the spaces. Use a different exclamation each time.

a. That's amazing! How's she doing?
b. Congratulations!
c. That's great! I knew you could do it.
d. That's disgusting!
e. No way!
f. You're kidding! What did you talk about?
g. Not again!
h. Oh no! That's awful!

1. _a_

2. _____

3. _____

4. _____

5. _____

6. _____

7. _____

8. _____

9 **Practicing Exclamations** Work in pairs. Student A should look at page 202. Student B should look at page 206.

Using Language Functions

GIVING AND ACCEPTING COMPLIMENTS

In many places, or cultures, people give compliments to make other people feel comfortable, to be friendly, or to start a conversation. Look at these examples of giving and accepting compliments.

Giving Compliments	Accepting Compliments
Maria, your English is really improving.	Thanks. You're very kind.
Excuse me. Who cut your hair? I really like it. I love the way you sing, Henry.	Thank you.
You have a beautiful home, Mrs. Johnson.	So do you./You do too.

10 Giving and Accepting Compliments Practice giving and accepting compliments with your classmates as follows: Student A gives a compliment to Student B. Student B accepts the compliment and gives a compliment to Student C. Continue until everyone has given and received a compliment. Here are some topics you can give people compliments on:

1. an item of clothing or jewelry

2. a hairstyle

3. something someone did

4. a change or improvement someone made recently

5. something a person does well

Part 2   Conversation: Arranging a Match

Before You Listen

 1 Prelistening Questions Before you listen, talk about social life and dating with a classmate.

1. Is dating common in your culture or circle of friends? If yes, how do you meet people to go on a date? If no, explain how you like to socialize with friends.

2. What do you think of "blind dates"? Do you know anyone who went on a blind date?

3. If you marry, how do you think you might meet your husband or wife?

4. Do you believe in love at first sight?

5. What are the most important things to look for in a husband or wife?

6. Would you trust your family members (parents or brothers and sisters) to select a husband or wife for you? Why, or why not?

Listen

2 Listening for Main Ideas Listen to the conversation between Tanya and Meena. As you listen to their conversation, answer the following questions.

1. What does Tanya want to do for her friend Meena?   *get a date*

2. Why does Meena say no to Tanya's suggestion?   *not allowed*

3. Does Tanya seem interested in learning about Meena's culture?   *yes what makes a good match*

3 **Taking Notes on Specific Information** Listen to the conversation again. This time, take notes about Meena's culture and its views on dating and marriage.

Ways to meet a husband: _family looking_ — _prof match maker_

For Meena, the right man must be: _god family share religious beliefs honest, kind, hard working_

Meena's view on love: _they won't m love takes time, can grow_

Possible advantages of this kind of marriage: _strong marriages_

After You Listen

4 **Summarizing Ideas** Work with a partner. Take turns explaining Meena's beliefs about a good marriage match. Use your notes from Activity 3 to help you.

5 **Discussing Dating Customs** Work in small groups. Talk about dating customs. Think about your own or your friends' experiences. Explain your answers.

1. In cultures where dating is popular, what age do you think is right for boys or girls to start dating?

2. Is it OK to ask someone you have just met out on a date?

3. Where do couples (married, or dating) in your culture go out together: to a movie? a restaurant? a nightclub? a concert?

4. When a couple goes out, who usually pays? Who should pay?

5. Do you think it is a good thing to date many different people before you get married? Why, or why not?

6. What do you think are some of the most usual, or unusual, ways or places that people in different cultures meet their future husbands or wives?

Culture Note

Dating in North America

When two people who have romantic feelings for each other go out together, their meeting is called a date. In the U.S. and Canada, boys and girls start dating around age 15. Often, people who are dating first met at school, at work, at a sports or music event, at a party, or at a club. Once in a while, a friend or relative arranges a date, and people meet for the first time at the time of the date. This is called a blind date.

Talk It Over

6 **Meeting Friends and Dates Online** Imagine that you just met the following six attractive single people at a party. Each wants to find someone to date. You are the "matchmaker." Read the notes about each person carefully. In small groups, talk about which pairs might make a good or bad match, and why.

Women	Matches?	Men
A: Lisa—22 Majored in biology; studied one year in Australia. Part-time job in pharmacy now, might continue for Masters degree. Independent, confident, funny. Loves shopping for expensive shoes.		X: Xiao (shao) Yong—25 Law major; very busy in new job at big law firm. Under a lot of stress Likes tennis, and just started golf. Enjoys spicy foods.
B: Marta—21 Studied Art History; is an artist who sells some of her paintings. Lives with her sister. Vegetarian who likes cooking healthy meals. Loves films, dancing, and travel. Very easygoing.		Y: Mo—24 Business major; might start MBA soon. Family has small export business. Serious—a bit old fashioned. Likes privacy and quiet places. His mother often cooks for him.
C: Anna—21 Accounting major with job offers at two strong companies. Shy, but friendly and kind. Likes reading and jogging. Gets take-out dinners often.		Z: Frank—23 Communications major, but is now learning animation. Part-time DJ, loves international dance music—doesn't earn much money. Likes trying new foods, but eats a lot of junk food when busy.

7 Filling Out a Questionnaire

Many new and popular Internet dating services try to help people find interesting people to date. New members usually fill out a questionnaire to explain who they are and what kind of person they'd like to meet. Then the service prepares a list of matches for them to look over and contact (or not).

Pretend that you are going to sign up with an online dating service, and follow these instructions.

1. Fill out the application, but don't write your real name at the top. Use an imaginary name. **You can answer truthfully, or have fun and make up pretend answers.** Your teacher will collect all the applications and put them on the board or wall.

2. The women in the class will read the applications from the men, and the men will read the applications from the women.

3. Choose the application of the person who seems the most interesting to you.

4. The teacher will hold up each application and ask, for example, "This application is from Mr. Cool. Can you all guess who this is?" (Students try to guess.) "Would you like to meet him? Well let's meet him now."

5. Finally, "Mr. Cool" will stand up and reveal his identity.

6. Repeat steps 4 and 5 for all the applications.

FindYourMatch.com

'User Name' (__not__ real name) _____ Age: _____ ❑ Male ❑ Female

ME:

School major or favorite class _____

Future plans or dreams (be accountant at big company, start a restaurant, get

married and have children, etc.): _____

_____

Good habits (very loyal, exercise daily, etc.): _____

_____

Bad habits (eat junk food, step on toes when dancing, etc.): _____

_____

Finish these sentences:

My friends say I am very . . . a) _____ b) _____

Two things that make me happy are . . . a) _____ b) _____

Two things that make me angry are . . . a) _____ b) _____

My hobbies and interests include . . . (video games, tennis, rap music, etc.)

_____

Three things I can't live without, are: (nice shoes, my cat, travel, religion, etc.)

1) _____ 2) _____ 3) _____

MY FUTURE DATE:

Should be _____ to _____ years old, and have these . . . :

Future plans or dreams (finish college, be president of a big company, open

---

a restaurant, get married and have children, make a lot of money, make a
movie, etc.): _____

_____

_____

_____

_____

_____

_____

Good habits: (very loyal, exercise daily, etc.): _____

_____

_____

_____

(Not have these) Bad habits: (eat junk food, watch too much TV, etc.):

_____

_____

_____

_____

Hobbies and interests such as (jazz music, cooking, snowboarding, etc.):

_____

_____

_____

_____

_____

_____

Getting Meaning from Context

TOEFL® iBT

Focus on Testing

Using Context Clues Many tests such as the TOEFL® iBT measure your academic listening and speaking abilities. This activity, and others in the book, will develop your social and academic communication abilities, and provide a foundation for success on a variety of standardized tests. Listen to five conversations that take place at a party.

1. Listen to the first part of each conversation. Then listen to the question.

2. Stop the recording and choose the best answer to each question.

3. In the **Clues** column, write the words that helped you choose your answer.

4. Start the recording again. Listen to the last part of the conversation to hear the correct answer.

Answers	Clues
1. (A) The man doesn't like the town. (B) The man is new in town. (C) The woman used to live in the town.	
2. (A) The office manager hurt his neck. (B) The man works with the woman. (C) The man and woman used to work together.	pain in the neck
3. (A) The woman doesn't want to go out with the man. (B) The woman never eats lunch. (C) The man is going to call the woman this weekend.	
4. (A) The man is worried about Tony. (B) The woman is worried about Tony. (C) Tony went home.	
5. (A) The man and the woman will leave the party in forty-five minutes. (B) The man and woman had a misunderstanding. (C) The man and woman came to the party together.	

Talk It Over

1 **Discussing Parties** Answer the following questions with a small group.

1. Describe a typical, enjoyable party for people in your age group. Think of the kind of parties you might go to. Include the following information.
   a. Where is the party held?
   b. What time does the party start?
   c. What food is served?
   d. What do people drink?
   e. What kind of entertainment is there?
   f. Do you bring a gift for the host?
   g. When does the party end?

2. Why do you think some young people drink, or like to get drunk? What is your opinion of this activity?

3. If someone drinks alcohol at a party, how does that person get home?

4. The poster below is from an advertising campaign from the state of Connecticut (CT). Have you seen posters of advertisements like this before? Do posters like this stop people from drinking and driving?

1 **Prelistening Discussion** Look at the advertisements for entertainment below and on page 177. Answer the questions with a small group.

1. What type of entertainment is each poster advertising?

> a movie   a pop music concert
>
> a classical music concert   a nightclub (or dance club)
>
> an opera

2. Discuss which of these things you might like to do tonight. Decide on one activity with your group.

3. Discuss which activity you chose with the class.

2 **Previewing Vocabulary** You will hear the underlined words in some phone conversations and messages. Listen to the underlined words. Then use the context presented here to guess what the words mean. Write a definition or description in the spaces.

Sentences	Definitions
1. **A:** What's showing at the Coronet theater tonight? **B:** A sci-fi movie with Tom Cruise. **A:** Tom Cruise in a sci-fi movie—sounds exciting! What are the show times? **B:** 4, 7, and 10.	sci-fi movie: show times:
2. **A:** Want to go see some live music at the Sunset Grill tonight? **B:** Who's singing? **A:** A woman named Sarah Waggoner. She's supposed to be great. **B:** OK. What does it cost? **A:** There's a cover charge of 15 dollars and you have to buy at least two drinks. **B:** Sorry, that's too expensive for me.	live music: cover charge:
3. When you buy tickets to entertainment events on the Internet, you often have to pay a service charge of two dollars or more. If you order tickets by phone, you can get them in the mail or you can pick them up at the box office: before the event begins.	service charge:
4. If you want to have dinner at a well-known restaurant, it's best to make a reservation before you go. If you don't have a reservation, you may have to wait for a long time when you get there.	make a reservation:

With a partner, role-play Conversations 1 and 2.

3 Taking Notes Jack and Ming plan to go out this weekend. Ming is making phone calls to get more information about three entertaining events. Listen to the calls and take notes on the important information.

Call 1

Event: _____

Location: _____

Show time(s): _____

Price of tickets: _____

Call 2

Place: _____

Entertainment tonight: _____

Cost: _____

Menu: _____

Reservations: _____
              (Number of people)   (Time)

Call 3

Place: _____

Band: _____

Date: _____

Price (total): _____

Remember to bring: _____

4 Using Vocabulary Discuss the following questions with a partner. Use the underlined vocabulary in your answers.

1. Do you like sci-fi (science fiction) movies? Give an example of a movie you enjoyed.

2. Do you ever go to nightclubs to hear live music? Tell about the last time you went. What was the cover charge to get into the club? Did you have to make a reservation?

3. Have you ever ordered tickets to an event by phone? What was the service charge? Did your tickets come by mail, or did you pick them up at the box office?

4. How can you find out the show times for an event you want to attend?

5 Role-Play Work in pairs. Student A should look at page 202. Student B should look at page 206.

Self-Assessment Log

Check the words you learned in this chapter.

Nouns
- ❏ box office
- ❏ cover charge
- ❏ graduation
- ❏ live music
- ❏ pre-med
- ❏ sales rep
- ❏ sci-fi movie
- ❏ service charge
- ❏ show times
- ❏ vacancy

Verbs
- ❏ be up to
- ❏ keep in touch
- ❏ make a reservation
- ❏ make sense

Adjectives
- ❏ good at
- ❏ terrific

Expressions
- ❏ on the road

Check the things you did in this chapter. How well can you do each one?

	Very well	Fairly well	Not very well
I can listen to and practice stress.	❏	❏	❏
I can talk about friends.	❏	❏	❏
I can express strong feelings with exclamations.	❏	❏	❏
I can give and accept compliments.	❏	❏	❏
I can take notes on a conversation.	❏	❏	❏
I can summarize my notes.	❏	❏	❏
I can talk about dating customs and parties.	❏	❏	❏
I can guess meanings from context.	❏	❏	❏
I can talk about going out to movies and clubs.	❏	❏	❏

Write about what you learned and liked in this chapter.

In this chapter,

I learned _____

_____

I liked _____

_____

10

Sports

In This Chapter

Conversation:	Explaining a Sport
Speech:	A Female Wrestler
Getting Meaning from Context:	Which Sport Is It?
Real-World Tasks:	Radio Sports Report

❝ I've failed over and over and over again in my life
and that is why I succeed. ❞

—Michael Jordan
American basketball player (1963–)

Connecting to the Topic

1 Look at the photo. What's happening?

2 What are your favorite sports to watch? Why?

3 What qualities do you think someone needs in order to become a successful athlete? Explain.

Before You Listen

 1 **Prelistening Questions** Look at the photo. Answer the questions with a partner.

1. What do you know about martial arts?

2. Why do people want to learn such sports?

3. What experience, if any, do you have with them?

▲ A woman practicing Karate

 2 **Previewing Vocabulary** Listen to the words and phrases from the conversation. Complete the sentences with the words and phrases.

Nouns	Verbs	
balance	focus	stretch
confidence	get in shape	warm up
flexibility	get into	

1. My uncle hasn't exercised for many years and he has gained a lot of weight.

   But now he wants to _____.

2. Some basketball players can jump and _____ their arms up to touch the basket.

3. Bicyclists need good _____ if they don't want to fall off their bikes.

4. Many young women who are shy often develop more _____ after they learn to play a sport well.

5. To do yoga or gymnastics, you need great _____ to move your body in difficult positions.

6. If you have a lot of fun doing a new sport, it's easy to _____ it.

7. To become a winner, you must concentrate your vision and effort in one direction. You really need to _____ on your goal.

8. Professional tennis players usually _____ for several minutes to get their bodies ready to start to play a match.

Listen

3 **Listening for Main Ideas** Ming, Peter, and Kenji are together to practice some martial arts. Close your book as you listen. Prepare to answer these questions:

1. What sport will Ming, Peter, and Kenji practice?

2. What part of the world does this sport come from?

3. What are some differences between the two sports they discuss?

4. How has this sport helped Ming?

Compare and discuss your answers with a partner.

▲ Kick

▲ Block

▲ Punch

4 **Listening for Details** Listen again if necessary. Write *T* if a statement is true and *F* if it is false.

_____ **1.** Ming is trying to teach her friends Karate.

_____ **2.** Tae Kwon Do uses more kicks than Karate does.

_____ **3.** Kenji doesn't have any experience with Karate.

_____ **4.** Peter isn't very interested in learning such sports.

Stress

5 **Listening for Stressed Words** Listen to the conversation again. Some of the stressed words are missing. During each pause, repeat the phrase or sentence. Then fill in the blanks with the words you hear.

Ming: OK guys. Let's _____ _____ and _____. We've got to work on _____ and _____.

Peter: So, Ming, when did you _____ _____ this Karate stuff?

Kenji: Karate's _____. Ming's showing us Tae Kwon Do, and it's Korean.

Peter: _____. So, what's the _____?

Ming: Tae Kwon Do uses _____ of different _____ moves. But Karate . . . well, Kenji, it sounds like _____ know something about Karate.

Kenji: Yeah—Karate uses more _____ and _____, too. Maybe you've seen guys break wooden _____ with punches. You know, like . . . I learned _____ when I was in _____.

Peter: That's _____. I wish _____ could do that. So, Ming, why did you get into Tae Kwon Do?

Ming: I had a Korean friend in _____ school, and he said it could help me get in _____ and _____ my confidence. So I _____ it, and I really liked it.

Peter: It looks like you _____.

Now read the conversation with two other classmates. Practice stressing words correctly.

Reductions

DROPPING THE "H" SOUND

The "h" sound is not pronounced when a word is:

    unstressed AND in the middle of a phrase

or

    unstressed AND at the end of a sentence

The "h" sound is often dropped in *pronouns,* and *have/has/had.*

    For example:

Unreduced "h"	**Dropped "h"**
Has he won yet?	Has 'e won yet?
I don't know how to find her.	I don't know how to find 'er.

In the following examples, the "h" is not dropped because it is in a stressed word:

    Can I **help** you?

    I **hope** so.

---

6 Listening for the Dropped "h" Listen to the following sentences. Repeat them after the speaker.

Unreduced Pronunciation	**Dropped "h" Pronunciation***
1. I don't know what to get her.	**1.** I don't know what to get 'er.
2. Give it to him.	**2.** Give it to 'im.
3. Is he winning?	**3.** Is 'e winning?
4. What's his team's name?	**4.** What's 'is team's name?
5. Where have you been?	**5.** Where 'uv you been?
6. Susan has finished her workout.	**6.** Susan 'as finished 'er workout.
7. He helped her get tickets.	**7.** He helped 'er get tickets.

7 Comparing Unreduced and Reduced Pronunciation The following sentences come from the conversation. Listen for the difference between the unreduced and reduced pronunciation. Repeat both forms after the speaker.

Unreduced Pronunciation	**Reduced Pronunciation***
1. We've got to work on balance.	We've gotta work on balance.
2. Why did you get into Tae Kwon Do?	Why didja get into Tae Kwon Do?
3. And he said it could help me . . .	An 'e said it could help me . . .
4. It looks like you succeeded.	It looks likeya succeeded.
5. I'm still working on it.	I'm still workin' on it.

---

* Note: The underlined forms are not acceptable spellings in written English.

8 **Listening for Reductions** Listen to the following conversation between roommates. You'll hear the reduced forms of some words. Repeat each sentence during the pause. Then write the unreduced forms of the missing words in the blanks.

Jane: Hi, Helen. Are _____ going out?

Helen: Yeah, I'm going to the football game. My brother's playing and I thought I'd watch _____. Do you _____ _____ come?

Jane: I really can't . . . I _____ _____ study. But can _____ do me a favor?

Helen: OK.

Jane: _____ _____ get me tickets for the girls' soccer game next Saturday? My cousin Sue just made the team.

Helen: Sure—that's so cool. What's _____ position?

Jane: I'm not sure—I'm _____ _____ call _____, and I can ask _____, if you want.

Helen: _____ don't have to—just wish _____ luck.

With a partner, read the conversation. Practice the reduced pronunciation.

After You Listen

9 **Reviewing Vocabulary** Discuss the following questions with a partner. Use the new vocabulary in your discussion.

1. What's your favorite sport, or game, and how did you <u>get into</u> it?

2. Why is it important to <u>warm up</u> before beginning to play a game or match?

3. Which activity do you think helps you <u>get in shape</u> the best: going dancing, playing ping pong, or racing cars?

4. What are a few sports for which you really need <u>flexibility</u> and you have to stretch a lot?

5. Can you think of a sport that especially requires very good <u>focus</u> and <u>balance</u>?

6. How can playing a sport build a person's <u>confidence</u>?

▲ Ping pong paddles and ball

▲ Going dancing

▲ Racing cars

Pronunciation

THE NORTH AMERICAN "T"

In some words, speakers of North American English pronounce the "t" between two vowels as a quick /d/ sound:

Karate's (kerahdeez) Japanese.

This pronunciation change does not happen in British English.

Contrast:

Words	North American English Pronunciation	British English Pronunciation
pretty	priddy*	pritty*
got it	goddit*	gottit*

*Note that the words marked with * are not correct written forms.

10 Listening for the North American "t" Listen and repeat the following examples.

1. We've gotta work on balance and flexibility. ("godda") ("flexibilidy")

2. It also helps you focus. ("id")

3. Let's get started ("starded")

11 Pronouncing the North American "t" Work in pairs. Student A should look at page 203. Student B should look at page 207.

Before You Listen

1 **Prelistening Questions** Before you listen, talk about sports with a partner.

1. Which sports are more popular among men than women? Why?

2. How much do you know about the sport of wrestling? For example, what are the rules, what are the different kinds, etc?

2 **Previewing Vocabulary** Listen to the underlined words from the speech. Then write the letter of the correct definition beside each sentence.

Sentences

1. _____ Our soccer team competed against another team and won.

2. _____ My roommate and I played a tennis match and then watched a soccer match on TV.

3. _____ John was so happy because he beat his father at a card game.

4. _____ We lost the basketball game because our opponents played much better.

5. _____ Nobody scored during the game, so the result was 0:0.

6. _____ Since the game was tied 2:2, they had to play overtime until one team finally won.

7. _____ Swimming is a great sport because you can participate as an individual or as a team member.

Definitions

a. to win against another player

b. the other player or team in a competition

c. to make points in a sport or game

d. to play a sport and try to win

e. one person, not a member of a group

f. a game or contest

g. extra time added at the end of a sports game

3 Taking Notes on Main Ideas Listen to the speech. Take notes in the space below. Focus on the main ideas about the speaker and her sport.

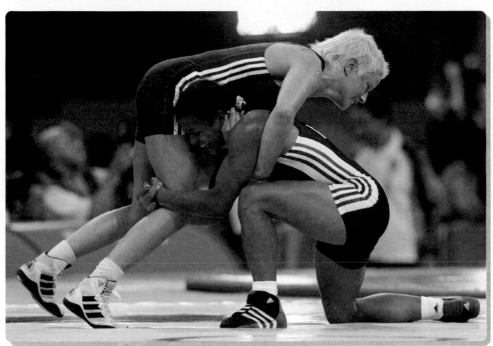

▲ France's wrestler Anna Gomis (blue) wrestles Ida Karlson from Switzerland.

Strategy

Hints for Taking Notes
It is easier to remember information if you organize your notes into an *outline*. An outline separates main ideas and details in a clear way with numbers and letters. An outline has key words and phrases—not complete sentences.

4 **Reviewing Notes** Look at your notes in Activity 3. Separate the main ideas from the details and write them in the outline below.

I. Introduction

   A. Info about Terri: _____

   B. Info about wrestling: _____

II. Why chose wrestling: _____

_____

III. Rules: _____

_____

_____

_____

IV. Why likes it: _____

_____

 5 **Listening for Specific Information** Listen again while you look at the outline. Make corrections or fill in missing information.

After You Listen

6 **Summarizing Ideas** Compare notes with a partner. Summarize the information in your outline. Based on your summary, work with a partner and role-play an imaginary interview with Terri.

Example

Reporter: When did you start wrestling?

Terri: When I was 12.

Reporter: Why did you choose this sport?

Terri: Because my brothers used to wrestle and I . . .

7 **Reviewing Vocabulary** Ask and answer the following questions with a partner. Use the underlined vocabulary in your answers.

1. Why do you think women wrestlers couldn't <u>compete</u> in the Olympics before 2004?

2. Do you prefer to compete in sports as an <u>individual</u> or as part of a team? Why?

3. In your opinion, should women compete only against each other or against both female and male <u>opponents</u> in the following sports? Why?

- swimming
- soccer
- wrestling
- golf
- running
- skiing

Using Language Functions

TALKING ABOUT SPORTS

With some sports, you can add *-ing* or *-er* to describe the activity or the athlete.

ACTION (verb)	SPORT (noun)	PERSON (noun)
wrestle	wrestling	wrestler
ice-skate	ice-skating	ice-skater
surf	surfing	surfer
box	boxing	boxer

Example *Surfing* is my favorite sport. I *surf* every summer. All my friends are *surfers*.

Some sports only have noun forms. These sports follow the verbs *play* or *do*.

Example play tennis   do gymnastics
            play volleyball   do karate

8 **Talking About Sports** Look at these photos. Describe each photo using the correct noun or verb.

Example These hockey players are playing hockey.

▲ Hockey

▲ Diving

▲ Snowboarding

▲ Yoga

Getting Meaning from Context

 1 Prelistening Questions Look at the pictures below. Name each sport and answer these questions with a partner.

1. Compare the sports in each group: how are they similar or different?
2. Which of these can you do without any equipment?
3. Which of these sports do you think is the oldest?

TOEFL® iBT

Focus on Testing

Using Context Clues Many tests such as the TOEFL® iBT measure your academic listening and speaking abilities. This activity, and others in the book, will develop your social and academic communication abilities and provide a foundation for success on a variety of standardized tests. Listen to people describe various sports.

1. Listen to each description.
2. Stop the recording after each description.
3. Choose the best answer for each item.
4. In the **Clues** column, write the words that helped you.

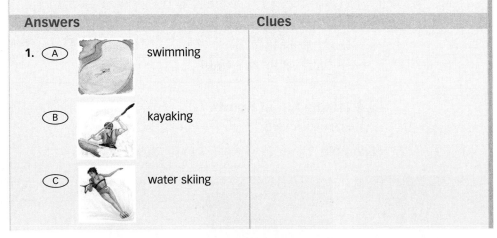

Answers	Clues
1. Ⓐ swimming	
Ⓑ kayaking	
Ⓒ water skiing	

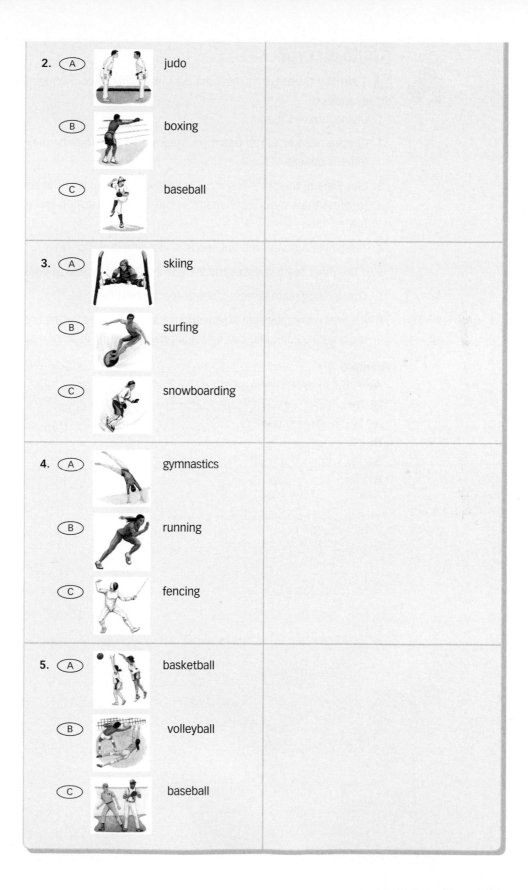

2. Ⓐ judo

   Ⓑ boxing

   Ⓒ baseball

3. Ⓐ skiing

   Ⓑ surfing

   Ⓒ snowboarding

4. Ⓐ gymnastics

   Ⓑ running

   Ⓒ fencing

5. Ⓐ basketball

   Ⓑ volleyball

   Ⓒ baseball

2 **Twenty Questions** Play the guessing game "Twenty Questions" by following these steps:

1. Divide into two teams.

2. Choose a player to represent your team. This person must think of a sport or a famous athlete.

3. Members of the other team ask Yes/No questions about the sport or athlete and try to guess the answer. Each member can ask one question and make one guess at his/her turn.

4. The player answers the questions with a simple Yes or No.

5. If the other team guesses the answer in 20 clues or less, it wins and gets one point.

6. The winning team selects a player for the next turn.

7. If a team can't guess in 20 questions (or guesses the wrong answer), the opposite team gets a point and can select another player to think of a sport or athlete.

Example

A: Is it a sport?

B: Yes.

A: Is it a winter sport?

B: No.

A: Do you need any special equipment?

B: Yes. . . .

1 Prelistening Questions Discuss these questions with a partner.

1. Which sports or games have you watched "live" at a stadium or other location? Which sports have you watched on television? Which way is better? Why?

2. Have you ever listened to a game on the radio? Is this enjoyable? Why, or why not?

3. Do you follow any sports, teams, or players through television news, newspapers, magazines, or the Internet? Explain.

2 Previewing Vocabulary Listen to the words below. Then test your understanding of the words. Working with a partner, describe or explain each picture by using the correct forms of the words under each picture. Check answers with classmates.

Nouns	Verbs	Adjective	Expressions
loser	lose/lost	close	It was a tie!
rival	win/won		It was a close game.
score			What was the score?
set			
tie			
winner			

Win/won/winner
lose/lost/loser
rival

close
the score
a tie

3 Sports News on the Radio Look at the chart about sports. Listen to the Faber College radio sports reporters. As you listen, fill in the missing information you hear about each game or sport.

Sport	Players or Teams	Results / Scores
Men's basketball	Faber vs. State College	Faber lost: 76 – 72
	Faber vs. Hamilton College	
		Won all 3 games: 1: 2: 21 – 18 3:
Tennis	Mary Johnson vs. _____	
Tournament		
Tennis	_____ vs. Lisa Kim	
Women's soccer		

GIVING AND UNDERSTANDING INSTRUCTIONS

When giving instructions, use signal words to make sure your explanation is clear.

Ask questions to make sure your listener understood you.

> First, . . .
> Start with . . .
> Then, . . .
> After that, . . .
> The last step is . . .

> Is this clear?
> Did you get that?
> Are you following me?

When following instructions, ask for clarification.

> I'm lost.
> I didn't get that.
> Wait. Can you say that again?
> Would you repeat that?

4 **Sports Instructions** Use the expressions from the list on page 197 as you play these games.

Game 1

1. Form groups (3 to 5 students). Each group writes a set of simple instructions, or rules, for playing a sport or game.

   Example (surfing)   First carry the board into the ocean. . . . Then lie down on the surfboard. . . . Next swim (or, paddle) out to some waves. . . . Turn around to the beach. . . . Now wait for a big wave. . . . Swim fast toward the beach. Finally, stand up on your surfboard.

2. Then cut up the instructions into separate sentences.

3. Give the mixed-up sentences to another group to put in correct order.

4. When you're done, check the answers.

Game 2

1. Form groups (3 to 5 students). With your group, write a set of instructions for playing a sport. Memorize the instructions. Each group slowly tells the instructions to the other groups, *without saying* the name of the sport.

2. The group that guesses the name of the sport first wins 1 point. After each group has explained their sport, the group with the most points wins.

   Example First, throw the ball up. Then hit it with your paddle. Try to hit the ball onto the table, then over the net. Next, the other player tries to hit the ball back to you. Continue to hit the ball over the net. If you can't hit it over the net, and onto the table, then you might lose a point (Answer: Ping Pong).

5 **Teaching or Coaching Your Classmates: Homework Project**

At Home:

Write down several simple steps for any sport you know. Practice explaining and showing these steps.

In Class:

If possible, bring in some sports equipment, like a ball or tennis racket, to help you describe your sport. Give instructions to try to teach your classmates the sport. Remember to check for understanding.

Learners: Remember to ask for help if instructions aren't clear.

Self-Assessment Log

Check the words you learned in this chapter.

Nouns	**Verbs**	**Adjectives**	**Expressions**
❏ balance	❏ beat	❏ close	❏ What was the
❏ confidence	❏ compete		score?
❏ flexibility	❏ focus	**Adverbs**	❏ It was a tie!
❏ individual	❏ get in shape	❏ overtime	❏ It was a close
❏ loser	❏ get into		game.
❏ match	❏ lose		
❏ opponent	❏ score		
❏ rival	❏ stretch		
❏ score	❏ warm up		
❏ set	❏ win		
❏ tennis match			
❏ tie			
❏ winner			

Check the things you did in this chapter. How well can you do each one?

	Very well	Fairly well	Not very well
I can listen to and practice stress and reductions.	❏	❏	❏
I can listen to and pronounce the North American "t."	❏	❏	❏
I can talk about sports.	❏	❏	❏
I can take notes on a speech.	❏	❏	❏
I can summarize my notes.	❏	❏	❏
I can guess meanings from context.	❏	❏	❏
I can give and understand instructions.	❏	❏	❏

Write what you learned and what you liked in this chapter.

In this chapter,

I learned _____

_____

I liked _____

_____

Pairwork Activities for Student A

Chapter 1 Part 1

8 Reviewing Vocabulary page 8

1. Questions: Ask the following questions. Your partner will choose the best response from his or her list.

    1. Do you think it is OK to stop by a friend's house without calling first?
    2. What classes are you going to take after this one?
    3. When did you come over from Taiwan?

2. Answers: Now change roles. Listen to your partner ask you three questions. Choose the correct response from the list below for each question.

    a. No kidding! You must be very healthy!
    b. Yi-Lun sounds Chinese to me. And Hyun? That sounds Korean.
    c. Some family members and school friends call me _____

Chapter 2 Part 3

2 Talking About Seasons page 35

Student A				
	Winter	**Spring**	**Summer**	**Fall**
Months	December–February		June–August	
Weather		warm		cool
			humid	cloudy
			sunny	
	snowy			
	wet			
	gray			

Chapter 5 Part 1

8 **Using Vocabulary** page 88

1. Questions: Ask the following questions. Your partner will choose the best response from his or her list.

   1. In what situations do you feel <u>stressed out</u>?

   2. In your community, can <u>landlords</u> <u>raise</u> the rent any time, as much as they want? Does the government control the rent?

   3. Is it <u>pretty</u> easy to find <u>vacancies</u> for apartments in your neighborhood? Why, or why not?

2. Answers: Now change roles. Listen to your partner ask you three questions. Choose the correct response for each question. (Use one or more choices inside the parentheses or use your own answer.)

   a. Yes, because (dormitory food is terrible, parents bought a new house, going to college)

   No, because (live with my family, like my roommates, rent is very low)

   b. Furnished (host family's house has furniture, dormitory has furniture, parents' house)

   Unfurnished (my first apartment, usually unfurnished in my town)

   c. (small size is convenient—easy to clean; too small—can't invite friends over, not enough room for all my stuff)

Chapter 5 Part 4

3 **Comparing Pictures** page 99

▲ Picture A

10 Practicing Exclamations page 167

1. Questions: You want to go to the movie *Gladiator Reborn*. Phone the theater and get some information about it. Your partner will choose the best response from his or her list.

Useful expressions

What time is _____ showing?   How long is the movie?

When does _____ start?   What's the address of the theater?

How much are the tickets?   Where can I park?

2. Answers: Now change roles. You work for Ticket Express, an agency that sells tickets for a variety of cultural events. Your partner will phone you to order tickets to the show, *The Lion King,* at the Greek Theater. Here is the information you will need:

Show time: 8:30 P.M.

Ticket prices: $20, $30, $50. The $20 tickets are sold out. There is a service charge of $2.50 for each ticket ordered by phone.

Ticket pickup: At the box office one hour before show time.

Useful expressions

The show begins at . . .   There is a service charge . . .

The (show) is sold out.   You can pick up your tickets at . . .

Chapter 9 Part 4

5 Role-Play page 178

Read your partner one statement or question from the list below. Your partner will respond with an appropriate exclamation. Then your partner will read one of his or her statements, and you will respond with an appropriate exclamation. Take turns.

1. I got 100% on the last grammar test.

2. Do you like my new haircut?

3. Yesterday my dog was hit by a car.

4. I got free tickets to the _____ concert.
   (Fill in the name of a rock group.)

5. (Make your own statement or question.)

11 Pronouncing the North American "t" page 187

1. Questions: Ask the following questions. Your partner will answer with a word containing the North American "t":

    1. When are you going to see the basketball game?

    2. Where was the Mexican soccer match?

    3. Do you think that swimmer is beautiful?

    4. Should I buy this sweater?

    5. I called my tennis partner, but she isn't home. What should I do?

2. Answers: Now change roles. Listen to and answer your partner's questions with one of these words or phrases:

    a British sport   better   hit it   mail it in   I try to play golf.

Pairwork Activities for Student B

8 **Reviewing Vocabulary** page 8

1. Answers: Listen to your partner ask you three questions. Choose the correct response from the list below.

   a. I came over to the United States three years ago.

   b. To be polite, it's better to call your friend before you stop by.

   c. After I take this English class, I want to take some business classes and maybe try to get an MBA.

2. Questions: Now change roles. Ask the following questions. Your partner will choose the best response from his or her list.

   1. What does your family call you?

   2. Can you believe I ran 10 kilometers this morning?

   3. My new classmates are Hyun, Roberto and Yi-Lun. Roberto sounds Spanish. Where do you think Hyun and Yi-Lun are from?

2 **Talking About Seasons** page 35

Student B				
	Winter	**Spring**	**Summer**	**Fall**
Months		March–May		September–November
Weather	cold		hot	
	rainy	cool		
	cloudy	rainy		windy
				rainy

Chapter 5 Part 1

8 Using Vocabulary page 88

1. Answers: Listen to your partner ask you three questions. Choose the correct response for each question.

    a. Yes, because (many new apartments, rent is very reasonable)

       No, because (rent is very high, not enough apartments, need help of agency)

    b. The landlord can raise the rent _____ (once a year, whenever he wants, only with government permission)

    c. Whenever I (move/pay bills/look for a roommate) I feel . . .

2. Questions: Ask the following questions. Your partner will choose the best response from his or her box.

    1. What are the advantages and disadvantages of a studio apartment?

    2. Are you planning to move out of your present home soon? Why or why not?

    3. When you first moved into your present home, was it furnished or unfurnished? Why?

Chapter 5 Part 4

3 Comparing Pictures page 99

▲ Picture B

10 Practicing Exclamations page 167

1. Answers: You work at the Sunset Theater. Your partner will call you for some ticket information. Use this information to answer your partner's questions. (If you don't know an answer, make something up.)

   Movie: *Gladiator Reborn*

   Location: Sunset Theater, at the corner of Sunset St. and King's Road

   Show times: 4, 7, and 10 P.M.

   Ticket prices: $6.00 before 5 P.M.; $10.00 after 5 P.M.

   Useful expressions

There's a show at . . .	We're located at . . .
Show times are . . .	Tickets cost . . .

2. Questions: Now change roles. You are going to call Ticket Express, an agency that sells tickets to sports and cultural events. You want to buy two tickets to the show, *The Lion King,* at the Greek Theater on the night of August 10.

   Useful expressions

I'd like to order . . .	Where can I pick up the tickets?
How much are the tickets?	What time does the show begin?
Do you have student tickets?	

5 Role-Play page 178

Read your partner one statement or question from the list below. Your partner will respond with an appropriate exclamation. Then your partner will read one of his or her statements, and you will respond with an appropriate exclamation. Take turns.

1. Somebody stole my brand-new bicycle.

2. I got accepted for next year at _____
   (Fill in the name of a university.)

3. What do you think of the food at _____?
   (Fill in the name of a terrible restaurant or place to eat.)

4. Today is my birthday.

5. (Make your own statement or question.)

11 Pronouncing the North American "t" page 187

1. Answers: Listen to and answer your partner's questions with a word or phrase containing the North American "t":

   pretty   call her later   try it on   Mexico City   Saturday

2. Questions: Now change roles. Ask your partner these questions:

   1. What do you try to do every weekend?
   2. What should I do with my completed application?
   3. What is the opposite of worse?
   4. What kind of game is cricket?
   5. What do players do with a golf ball?

Audioscript

Chapter 1 Academic Life Around the World

Part 1 Conversation: Meeting New Friends

3 **Listening for Main Ideas** page 5

4 **Listening for Details** page 5

5 **Listening for Stressed Words** page 6

Jack: Hi. How are you doing?

Peter: Hi. You're . . . Jack, right?

Jack: Yeah. And, sorry, you're . . . ?

Peter: Peter. Peter Riley.

Jack: Oh, yeah, we met on campus last week. Peter, this is my friend, Ming Lee. She's just moved into the building.

Peter: Hi, Ming Lee.

Ming: Nice to meet you. You can just call me Ming. Lee's my last name.

Peter: Oh. Ming. That sounds . . .

Ming: Chinese.

Peter: Oh. So, you're from . . .

Ming: . . . from San Francisco. My parents came over from Hong Kong before I was born.

Peter: Oh, that's cool. Actually, uh, I was thinking of taking Chinese this term. Maybe you could help me.

Ming: Well, my Chinese really isn't very good . . .

Jack: Uh, listen, Peter. We're really hungry. Do you want to get something to eat with us?

Peter: Sorry, I can't. I have to go meet my new roommate.

Jack: Oh, OK. Well, stop by sometime. I'm up in 212.

Peter: Hey, I'm on the same floor. I'm in 220.

Jack: No kidding . . .

Peter: Well, nice meeting you, Ming. I'm sure I'll see you guys soon.

Ming and Jack: See you later.

7 Listening for Reductions page 8

1. How are you feeling?

2. See you in an hour.

3. Jack, do you want to eat at the cafeteria?

4. When do you have to meet your roommate?

9 Distinguishing Among -s Endings page 9

1. plays	**6.** phones
2. misses	**7.** washes
3. hopes	**8.** summarizes
4. stops	**9.** mothers
5. drives	**10.** puts

Part 2 Presentation: School Orientation

3 **Listening for Main Ideas** page 13

4 **Listening for Specific Information** page 14

Hello, everybody. Welcome to the American Language Center. I'm Gina Richards, your academic advisor. You can all just call me Gina. I know today is your first day at our school, so you're probably a little nervous and maybe a little shy, too. So, I want to tell you right at the beginning: if you don't understand something, please ask questions. OK? And listen very carefully because we're going to give you a lot of important information—information that will make your experience here enjoyable and useful. OK, here we go.

Let me tell you about the plan for today. There are three things on your schedule. First, you will take a placement test. This test will measure your English level. You'll take a reading, grammar, and composition test. Oh, and also listening. A listening test. The whole placement test takes three hours.

Next, you will meet in small groups, with a teacher, for an orientation. This orientation meeting will be about important things you need to know, like where to buy your books, what types of classes you'll have, how to find a roommate, things like that. This is where you can ask a lot of questions.

Then, finally, this afternoon, you will take a campus tour. We'll show you the main buildings where your classrooms are; you'll see some of the sports facilities, you know, the tennis courts, the swimming pool, places like that; and you'll also visit the library and the computer lab. I think you'll be surprised how large and how beautiful our campus is. All right. Are there any questions before we begin?

Part 3 Strategies for Better Listening and Speaking

Focus on Testing: Using Context Clues
page 15

Part 1
Peter: Let's get a medium with extra cheese and pepperoni on it.
Ming: Can we get mushrooms and tomatoes, too?
Kenji: I don't care. Just get a large one 'cause I'm really hungry.

Question 1: Where are the students?

Peter: This restaurant has got the best pizza on campus!

Part 2
Kenji: Yeah, they told me about this place at the orientation. So, Ming, how are your classes going?
Ming: Pretty good. Well, my chemistry class is a little boring. Professor Murphy knows the subject, but he's not a good teacher. Last week

he was sick, and his T.A. was teaching the class. She was much better. This T.A. spends a lot of time answering our questions and correcting our homework.

Question 2: What do you think "T.A." means?

Kenji: Teaching assistants aren't common in Japanese universities. The professors teach all the classes.

Part 3
Peter: Really?
Kenji: Uh huh. I was very surprised when I first came here. You know what else is unusual for me? All the facilities. I mean, the swimming pool, five tennis courts, the museum, even a post office! Faber College doesn't look like the college campus where I come from.

Question 3: What does Kenji think about the Faber College campus?

Kenji: It's completely different.

Part 4
Kenji: Speaking of tennis courts, I want to play tomorrow. Can I just go there or do I need to . . .

Peter: You need to make a reservation. Just call the tennis center and give them your ID number. You know, your student ID. They'll give you a reservation number. The office is open between 8 A.M. and 5 P.M.

Question 4: How can students make reservations for a tennis court?

Ming: Here's the phone number for reservations.

Part 5
Peter: Hey, Jack and I already have a court for tomorrow afternoon. Do you guys want to play doubles with us?
Kenji: Sounds good to me. Can you come Ming?
Ming: Yeah. I have a class 'til 2:00. Let's meet there at 2:30.

Question 5: What are the students going to do tomorrow?

Kenji: You mean, meet at the tennis court, right?
Peter: Uh huh. See you there.

Part 4   Real-World Tasks: Telephone Messages

1   Listening to Telephone Messages
page 18

Example:

Outgoing Message: Hi. You have reached 555-0121. Sorry, but we can't come to the phone right now. If you want to leave a message for Peter, press one. If you want to leave a message for Kenji, press two. We'll call you back as soon as we can.

Linda: Kenji, this is Linda from Dr. Brown's office. I'm calling to change your appointment. Unfortunately, Dr. Brown can't see you at two o'clock on Tuesday. But I can give you an appointment for Wednesday at 2:00. I hope that's convenient for you. Please let us know. Call us at 555-0162.

Message 1

Kelly: Kenji, this is Kelly from your math class. Remember me? I'm calling about this week's homework. I'm still sick and will probably stay home until Monday. So, like, uh, can you call me at 555-0149? Any time before 11:00 is OK. Thanks.

Message 2

Bud: Hi, Peter, it's Bud. Listen, want to go to a concert Saturday? It's a Latin jazz band, I think. My cousin has a couple of free tickets. Give me a call today if you're interested. I'm at Sheri's house, and her number is, uh, 555-0126. Or call me on my cell. The concert starts at eight-thirty, by the way. Talk to you later.

Message 3

Mrs. Henry: This is Mrs. Henry from the international student office, returning Kenji Suzuki's call. I'm sorry, but we still don't have your papers ready. Please check back next week; just call the main number and, uh, I'm at extension 4745.

Message 4

Don: Uh, yes, uh, this is the research library calling. Peter Riley, we have a biology book with your name and this phone number in it. If it's yours, you can pick it up at the front desk; just show your student identification. Ask for Lisa or Don.

Message 5

Kevin: Hello, Peter? Uh, my name is Kevin Potter. My advisor gave me your number; she said you work with students in math, and I need help studying for my midterm exam. Can you let me know if you're available and, uh, how much you charge for tutoring? My number is 555-0118. Thanks. Bye.

Message 6

Man: Kenji, this is Honda World Service calling. Your car's fixed. Please pick it up by 5:00 today. As we discussed, the charges came to $175.

3   Calling for Information   page 20

Ming: Hi, I'm calling to get a parking permit. Is parking lot nine available?

Admin: Yes, it is. What's your name, please?

Ming: Ming Lee. My first name is M-I-N-G.

Admin: M-I-N-D?

Ming: No. M as in mother, I as in India, N as in Nancy, and G as in girl. My last name is spelled L-E-E. That's L as in little, E-E.

Admin: OK, got it. Address?

Ming: 3251 Washington Street.

Admin: Day-time phone number?

Ming: Uh, 555-0103.

Admin: OK. What's the year and make of your car?

Ming: 2004 Toyota Camry.

Admin: License plate?

Ming: AWJ 130

Admin: One thirty or one thirteen?

Ming: One, three, oh.

Admin: OK. That'll be $210 for the semester or $420 for the year.

Ming: I just need it for the fall semester.

Admin: All right. So, just send in your payment for $210, and we'll send you a permit for lot number nine.

Ming: Great. Thank you very much.

Admin: You're welcome.

Ming: Bye.

Chapter 2 Experiencing Nature

Part 1   Conversation: Vacation Plans

3 **Listening for Main Ideas** page 25

4 **Listening for Details** page 26

5 **Listening for Stressed Words** page 26

Peter: Wow. Look. It's raining cats and dogs—again! I hate this weather. When does winter break start?

Jack: Winter break? It's only October.

Peter: I know, but I'm sick of studying. I want to go someplace warm and lie on the beach for a week. Someplace where it's sunny and dry. Florida or Hawaii, maybe?

Jack: Yeah. Where we can go swimming and snorkeling and get a great tan. Now that's my idea of a perfect vacation.

Ming: Not mine. I can't swim very well, and I don't like lying in the sun.

Peter: Oh, yeah? How come?

Ming: I don't know. I just prefer the mountains, especially in winter. I love snowboarding. In fact I'm planning to go to Bear Mountain with some friends in December. Do you guys want to come?

Jack: No thanks. I went there last year. I was freezing the whole time. Anyway, I don't know how to ski very well. Last year I fell about a hundred times.

Ming: Peter, how about you?

Peter: Sorry, I'm like Jack. I don't want to go anyplace where it's below 70 degrees.

Jack: By the way, what's the weather forecast for tomorrow?

Ming: The same as today. Cloudy, cold, and a 90 percent chance of rain.

Jack: Oh, no! I left my umbrella at the library.

Ming: You can borrow mine. I've got an extra one.

7 **Listening for Reductions** page 27

Jack: Hi, Ming. Hi, Peter.

Ming and Peter: Hey, Jack.

Ming: What's happening?

Jack: I'm going to the campus recreation center. Do you want to come?

Ming: What are you going to do there?

Jack: Well, it's a nice day. We can swim and lie in the sun.

Ming: Thanks, but I don't want to go. I'm too tired.

Jack: How about you, Peter?

Peter: I can't. I've got to stay at home and study. Maybe tomorrow.

9 **Distinguishing Between *Can* and *Can't*** page 29

1. She can't swim very well.

2. Michael can drive.

3. The boys can cook.

4. I can't find his phone number.

5. Kenji can't speak Spanish.

6. He can speak Japanese.

7. I can't understand him.

8. Peter can come with us.

9. She can't take photographs in the rain.

10. Herb can play tennis very well.

Part 2   Story: Camping

3 **Listening for Main Ideas** page 31

4 **Taking Notes on Specific Information** page 31

Manager: You're all wet and muddy. What happened to you?

Woman: You're not going to believe this! It's the most incredible thing! It all started when we decided to go hiking this morning.

Man: Yeah, the weather was sunny and clear when we got up. So we put on shorts and

T-shirts and went hiking. Half an hour later it started raining cats and dogs!

Woman: So we hiked back to our tent as fast as we could. We couldn't wait to change into dry clothes.

Man: Right. But when we went into our tent, we couldn't find our clothes! So we went back outside to look around. And then we saw the craziest thing. Two great big brown bears came out of the woods, and guess what? They were wearing our clothes!

Manager: Aw, come on. That's impossible! What do you mean, the bears were wearing your clothes?

Man: Well, one bear had my T-shirt around his neck. And the other one had Mary's pants over his head. We still don't know where the rest of our clothes are!

Manager: [laughing]

Woman: I know it sounds funny, but we were so scared! Those bears were big! And now we have a big problem.

Manager: What's that?

Woman and Man: We don't have any dry clothes to wear!

Part 3 Strategies for Better Listening and Speaking

Focus on Testing: Using Context Clues
page 35

Conversation 1

A: Nice weather we're having.

B: Yes. Isn't it a nice surprise? At this time it's usually much cooler and raining already.

A: Well, this weather will probably end soon; all the leaves on the trees are brown, and the nights are getting cold.

Conversation 2

A: Take your coat; it's freezing outside.

B: Nah, I'm only going to the corner store. I'll be back in five minutes.

A: I'm telling you, it's in the low thirties out there. Do you want to get sick?

Conversation 3

A: How do you like all this rain?

B: Well, it's good for the trees and flowers.

A: Yes, it's nice to see the leaves coming back on the trees again.

B: Yeah, and I'm glad the snow is all gone.

Conversation 4

A: Is it hot enough for you?

B: Whew . . . it sure is. I don't mind the heat so much. It's the humidity that bothers me. Look, I'm all wet.

A: Me too. Let's go get a cold drink somewhere.

B: Yeah, someplace with air conditioning.

Conversation 5

A: Ah, this is the life. No traffic, no worries. Just lie here and enjoy doing nothing.

B: Honey, your back is turning red. If you're not careful, you're going to get sunburned.

A: Could you put some sun screen on my back?

Part 4 Real-World Tasks: Weather

1 Listening for Temperatures page 36

Conversation 1

A: What's the weather like today?

B: Hot and humid and about ninety-five degrees.

Conversation 2

A: I'm going to take a swim. Want to come?

B: Is the pool heated?

A: Sure. It's probably over eighty degrees.

Conversation 3

A: How was your skiing holiday?

B: Great! The weather was in the thirties and we had perfect snow conditions.

Conversation 4

A: Let's go for a walk.

B: What's it like out?

A: About forty degrees, but the wind has stopped.

B: Thanks, but I think I'll stay inside where it's warm.

Conversation 5

A: It's a hundred and three in here! Why don't you turn on the air conditioning?

B: It's broken.

Conversation 6

A: How was the weather in Europe this summer?

B: Just lovely. Hot, but never over thirty degrees.

A: Thirty? Oh, you mean Celsius.

Conversation 7

A: What's wrong?

B: It's thirteen below outside and I can't find my gloves.

A: Here. Use mine. I have an extra pair.

Conversation 8

A: Did you check the weather forecast?

B: Yeah. It's supposed to be in the high seventies this weekend.

A: The seventies? I guess we can forget about skiing.

4 Listening to a Weather Forecast

page 37

This is the National Weather Service report at 5:00 in the afternoon, Friday. The forecast for the Bear Mountain area is partly cloudy with some showers through the night, clearing by early morning. The high today was sixty-one degrees; overnight lows will be in the mid-fifties. Tomorrow's highs will be in the sixties with fair skies continuing throughout the day. Temperatures will drop Saturday night to a chilly low of forty-five degrees. Sunday will continue fair, warming up to a high temperature of seventy degrees. Sunday night lows will get down below fifty again. There will be a fifty percent chance of rain on Monday.

Chapter 3 Living to Eat, or Eating to Live?

Part 1 Conversation: Shopping for Food

3 Listening for Main Ideas page 43

4 Listening for Details page 43

5 Listening for Stressed Words page 44

Andrew: Well, I got a few groceries that aren't on the list.

Nancy: I can see that! We're not shopping for an army, you know.

Andrew: I always do this when I'm hungry.

Nancy: Well, let's see what you have here.

Andrew: Some nice, fresh strawberries for only $1.79 a pound.

Nancy: Well, that's fine. They always have nice produce here. But why do you have all these cookies?

Andrew: Don't you like them?

Nancy: Oh, I don't know . . . I hope you got a box of tofu.

Andrew: I think I forgot. Where's the aisle with the Asian foods, again?

Nancy: Aisle three.

Andrew: I'll go get it.

Nancy: Wait—this steak you got looks really expensive!

Andrew: Well, it isn't. It's on sale for just $3.99 a pound.

Nancy: And what's this? More ice cream? We already have a quart at home. Why don't you put it back? Meanwhile, I'll get in line right here.

Cashier: I'm sorry, Miss; this is the express line, and it looks like you've got more than ten items. Oh, and we don't take checks here.

7 Listening for Reductions page 45

Customer: Waiter?

Server: Yes sir. Do you know what you want?

Customer: Do you have the spaghetti with mushroom sauce tonight?

Server: Yes, we do.

Customer: Well, are the mushrooms fresh or canned?

Server: They're fresh, and the sauce has lots of them.

Customer: Great, I'll have that.

Server: Do you want a glass of wine?

Customer: I don't know. Why don't you recommend something?

Server: I can suggest a nice Italian red.

9 Distinguishing between Teens and Tens page 46

1. We waited in line for 30 minutes.

2. My sister is 14 years old.

3. We've lived in this city for 15 years.

4. 60 people came to the party.

5. The groceries cost 70 dollars.

6. There are 18 students in the class.

7. I live 90 miles from my parents.

10 Listening for Teens and Tens page 47

1. This turkey weighs 14 pounds.

2. The market is open until 10:30.

3. We spent $40 on groceries yesterday.

4. This milk is good until November 13th.

5. Those peaches cost $1.90 a pound.

6. Everything in this store is about 15 percent cheaper today.

7. I'm having a big party this weekend. I need 30 bottles of mineral water.

8. The store will close in 15 minutes.

9. By using this coupon, you can save 70 cents on this ice cream.

10. Canned vegetables are in aisle 19.

Part 2 Advice Show: Healthy Eating

3 Listening for Main Ideas page 50

4 Taking Notes on Specific Information page 50

Bob: Hi, everyone, I'm Bob.

Pam: And I'm Pam, and this show is all about "Eating Right!"

Bob: You know, Pam, with people so busy today, they don't have a lot of time to shop or plan what to eat.

Pam: That's true, but healthy eating might just give you a longer and happier life! So here are some things we all should think about regarding our diet.

Bob: First, eat lots of fruits and vegetables. Why? Well, they're a good source of vitamins, and minerals. . . .

Pam: Right, and they're a good source of fiber, too. Also, they're almost all low in calories and fat, and eating them may help protect you against cancer. So, put an apple or a banana in your lunchbox, or have a carrot for a snack— skip those potato chips.

Bob: That's right. Fruits make a great desert— you don't need all those sugary sweets and drinks, cookies, cakes, candies, sodas.

Pam: You bet you don't. So a second point to remember: too much sugar in your diet can lead to health problems like weight gain, tooth decay—that's trips to your dentist . . .

Bob: Owww! Or even diabetes, and that's serious!

Pam: Now the third thing we want you to think about is reducing the fat you eat.

Bob: Uh huh. Cutting down on the fat in our diets would be good for many of us.

Pam: So true. It can help us lose weight.

Bob: Or *not gain* weight in the first place.

Pam: And it can lower our chance of getting heart disease, and cancer, too.

Bob: So cut back on all those hamburgers, cheeseburgers, French fries . . .

Pam: And chips—they're full of fat. . . .

Bob: And salt. Oh, I don't want to forget our

fourth suggestion: Eat more whole grains. You'll get plenty of fiber, vitamins, and minerals from them.

Pam: You mean, like, brown rice and whole wheat?

Bob: That's it. They're much healthier than white bread, white rice, and things like that.

Pam: Finally you don't want to drink too much coffee. Coffee can make you nervous, and keep you awake at night. Or even affect your heart— but we'll talk about that on another show. . . .

Part 3   Strategies for Better Listening and Speaking

Focus on Testing: Using Context Clues
page 53

Conversation 1

Server: Good evening. My name is Pierre. Would you like a something to drink?

Bob: No, thanks. But we would like to order some appetizers.

Server: Certainly, here are your menus. Our specials tonight are lemon chicken and fresh broiled swordfish.

Question 1: The speakers are in a . . .

Susan: This is such a beautiful restaurant, Bob. Thanks for bringing me here.

Conversation 2

Felipe: Why don't we sit at the counter? There aren't any free tables.

Salim: Fine.

Waitress: Coffee?

Felipe: Yes.

Salim: Yes, please.

Waitress: I'll be right back to take your order.

Question 2: The speakers are in a . . .

Felipe: This is my favorite diner. The prices are low and the service is great.

Conversation 3

A: These salads look great. Do you want one?

B: No, I want a hot dish from over there.

Server: Yes, what would you like?

A: Is that mushroom soup?

Server: No, it's bean soup.

A: How much is it?

Server: It's two dollars a bowl. You pay down there at the cashier.

Question 3: The speakers are in a . . .

B: I hear this cafeteria is open all night.

Conversation 4

Server: May I take your order?

John: I'll have two burritos, no onions, and two small Cokes.

Server: For here or to go?

John: For here. Oh, and an order of nachos.

Server: That'll be eight dollars.

Question 4: The speakers are in a . . .

John: I know fast food is fattening, but I really love it.

Part 4   Real-World Tasks: Recipies and Regional Foods

2 Taking Notes on a Recipe   page 56

Tom: To make French toast for four people, here's what you'll need: two eggs, one cup of milk, one-half teaspoon of salt, and about a tablespoon of butter. Have you got all that?

First, beat the eggs, milk, and salt with a fork for a minute until they're well mixed.

Then melt the butter in a frying pan.

While the butter is melting, dip eight slices of bread into the egg mixture.

Then, when the butter is hot, fry the bread slices until they're golden brown.

Serve them on a warm plate with butter and syrup or jam.

6 Regional Foods page 59

Look at the map of the United States and Canada. As you hear the name of each food, write it on the map in the place where it is popular.

Paula: Vancouver, in Western Canada, has delicious Chinese food because there are many Chinese immigrants in that part of Canada. And Vancouver has great fish—like salmon.

San Francisco also has excellent Chinese and Japanese restaurants. Oh and the bread in San Francisco is really special. Just north of San Francisco there are two little towns called Napa and Sonoma. That's where they make some wonderful California wine.

Now, if you drive to Texas, be sure to eat some Mexican food. It's very spicy, but so delicious. In the Midwest, the middle of the United States, you can find terrific cheese in Wisconsin. And don't forget to have a steak in Chicago. The beef is very good there.

If you drive to the Northeast, try to visit Maine to taste the seafood. Lobster is fantastic. And nearby, in Montreal, Canada, the French food is fabulous. Oh, and if you decide to go down south to Georgia, fried chicken is very popular. And in Florida, of course, you'll find the best oranges.

Chapter 4 In the Community

Part 1 Conversation: In the City

3 Listening for Main Ideas page 66

4 Listening for Details page 66

5 Listening for Stressed Words page 66

Kenji: Peter, are you going downtown today?
Peter: Uh-huh. Why?
Kenji: Can you give me a ride? I have to run some errands.

Peter: Where do you need to go?
Kenji: Uh, a lot of places. First, I have to go to the bank. Could you drop me off at the corner of King Boulevard and Second Avenue?
Peter: King and Second? Oh, sure. I know where that is. But why are you going to the bank? Why don't you use the ATM machine on campus?
Kenji: 'Cause my debit card isn't working; I've got to get a new one. And the cleaner's is next door to the bank. I have to pick up some clothes there anyway.
Peter: Why don't you use the laundry room here in the building?
Kenji: I'm not picking up laundry. It's dry cleaning. By the way, is there a computer repair shop near there? I need to drop off my laptop.
Peter: Computer repair? Oh, yeah. There's a Good Buy across the street from the bank. They fix computers there.
Kenji: Oh, that's convenient. So what are you going to do downtown?
Peter: I'm going to the courthouse. I've got to pay a traffic ticket.
Kenji: No kidding! I have to pay a ticket, too. I just got a ticket last week.
Peter: But, Kenji, you don't drive!
Kenji: I know. I got a ticket for jaywalking!
Peter: Really?!
Kenji: Yeah. I didn't know it's illegal to cross in the middle of the street!

7 Listening for Reductions page 68

A: Do you know where Central Library is?
B: Sure. You have to take Bus number 9.
A: Could you walk with me to the bus stop?
B: I'm sorry. I don't have time 'cause I've got to do a lot of things.
A: Oh. Then can you just give me directions to the bus stop?
B: Are you kidding? It's right there across the street.

Part 2 Conversation: Comparing Cities and Towns

3 Listing for Main Ideas page 73

4 Taking Notes on Specific Information page 74

Peter: Phew . . . I'm glad I don't live downtown. The traffic is terrible. I have a headache from the noise and all the smog.

Ming: You think our downtown is bad? Ask Kenji about Tokyo.

Kenji: Yeah, Tokyo is noisier and much more crowded.

Ming: Yeah, and I hear the smog's worse, too.

Kenji: That's right.

Peter: So, I guess you don't miss *that,* huh?

Kenji: Well, I don't miss *those* things. But a big city like Tokyo can be very exciting.

Peter: Yes, I'm sure that's true. But I prefer the peace and quiet of a small town like ours.

Kenji: Yeah, I like it here, too. The people are friendlier and things are cheaper.

Ming: Small towns can be so conservative and boring. When I graduate, I want to live in a big city like New York or Chicago. You can make more money there, too.

Peter: Yeah, but it's more dangerous there.

Ming: Yeah, that's a disadvantage. But there are also lots of advantages.

Peter: Like what? The long lines at the bank or in the stores?

Ming: Waiting in line doesn't bother me. I really love shopping in the city. You can find anything.

Kenji: Great! Then next time we need something downtown, we'll send *you.*

Part 3 Strategies for Better Listening and Speaking

Focus on Testing: Using Context Clues page 75

Conversation 1

A: Next, please.

B: I'd like to cash this.

A: Sure. Don't forget to sign the back. Do you have an account here?

B: Not at this branch.

A: Then I'll have to see your identification.

Question 1: Where are the speakers?

B: By the way, how late is this bank open?

Conversation 2

A: Excuse me. Do you stop at Third and Highland?

B: Yes, ma'am . . . Passengers, please move to the rear.

A: Could you tell me when we get there?

B: Sure. I'll let you know.

Question 2: Where is the woman?

A: Is the bus always this crowded?

Conversation 3

A: Can I help you?

B: Yes, I've got four shirts here and two pairs of pants and a jacket. I'm leaving town in a few days, so can I pick them up tomorrow?

A: We can have the pants ready, but the shirts won't be back until Wednesday morning.

B: Well, OK. Oh, and don't forget to take out this coffee stain.

Question 3: Where are the speakers?

A: No problem. We're the best dry cleaners in town.

Conversation 4

A: Fill out this application and wait in that line for your eye test.

B: About how long will this take?

217

A: Well, you'll have to take a fifteen-minute road test, and the written test also takes fifteen minutes. But you may have to wait in line a long time for your picture.

Question 4: What is the young man doing?

B: Will you send me my driver's license, or do I have to pick it up in person?

Conversation 5

A: Will this get to New York in two days?

B: Only if you send it express mail.

A: OK. I'd like to do that.

B: All right. Anything else?

A: Yes. A book of stamps, please.

B: Fine, that's, uh, sixteen dollars and sixty cents, please.

Question 5: Where are the speakers?

A: Is this post office open on Saturdays?

Part 4 Real-World Tasks: Directions

2 Following Directions page 79

Peter: Excuse me. Is there a bank near here?

Man: There's one four or five blocks from here. Walk north on Newbury Boulevard to First Street; turn right on First. At the second block, turn left and look for the bank on the right side of Walnut Street just before Cherry Lane.

You are at location C. Continue to the next place from here.

Peter: Excuse me, ma'am. I'm trying to find a big department store nearby.

Woman: Oh, there's one on the corner of Newbury and Cherry. Just walk down Cherry two blocks and turn left. Then you'll see it on the left.

You are at location A. Continue to the next place from here.

Peter: Could you tell me where King's Books is? I hear it's a great bookstore.

Man: King's Books? Oh, yes. They've got great stuff. Do you know how to get to Washington Boulevard?

Peter: I think so. I go out on First Street and turn right.

Man: Nope. Turn left. Washington's the first street. Turn right on Washington and follow it a couple of blocks to Columbus Street. Turn left and cross Walnut Street. On the left side you'll see a barbershop and then a market. Walk between them, and you'll find the bookstore in back.

You are at location F. Continue to the next place from here.

Peter: Can you recommend a Chinese restaurant near here?

Woman: Sure. Chow's has good Chinese food.

Peter: How do I get there?

Woman: Go out to Walnut Street and go up to Second Street. Walk west, cross Washington Boulevard, and the restaurant is across from Mort's Gym.

Peter: So it's on the south side of the street?

Woman: That's right.

You are at location E. Continue to the next place from here.

Peter: Is there a concert at Lowe Auditorium tonight?

Man: I think so.

Peter: How do I get there?

Man: Are you driving?

Peter: No, I'm walking.

Man: Turn right and walk all the way to McMillan Road. Then make a left and go straight a block or two. The auditorium is on the corner of Cherry Lane and McMillan.

You have arrived at location H. Stop and relax.

4 Listening for Directions on the Phone page 80

Conversation 1

A: Metro Bus Company.

B: Hello. I need to go to the airport from Main Street.

A: Main Street and what?

B: Main and Grant.

A: OK. What time do you have to be at the airport?

B: At six o'clock.

A: Take bus thirty-three at four-fifty at the

corner of Main and Grant. Get off at Airport Boulevard. That's two blocks from the airport.

B: So it's bus number thirty-three at four-fifty; and I get off at . . .

A: Airport Boulevard.

B: Thank you very much.

Conversation 2

A: Bus information. Tom speaking.

B: I want to go to Salem. Is there a bus at around nine in the morning?

A: Just a minute . . . There's one at eight-fifty, leaving from the Hilton Hotel.

B: I see. What's the fare?

A: It's $7 one way.

B: How long does it take?

A: About forty minutes.

B: Thanks.

Conversation 3

A: Metro Bus Company. May I help you?

B: How can I get to 1800 Orange Street?

A: From where?

B: From Hollywood Boulevard. Hollywood and Temple.

A: Get on bus number 102 at the corner of Hollywood and Temple. Get off at Madison Avenue and Orange, then walk two blocks north on Orange.

B: How often does the bus run?

A: Ah, let's see. Bus 102 runs, uh, every six minutes.

B: Every six minutes? That's great. Thanks.

Chapter 5 Home

Part 1 Conversation: Finding the Right Apartment

3 Listening for Main Ideas page 85

4 Listening for Details page 86

5 Listening for Stressed Words page 86

Beth: I'm so stressed out. My landlord just raised my rent. I think I'll have to move.

Ming: Really? You know, my building has some vacancies. It's a pretty nice place, and it's just ten minutes from campus.

Beth: Oh yeah? How much is the rent for a studio?

Ming: There are no studio apartments in our building. My neighbor just moved out of a one-bedroom. He paid $850 a month, I think.

Beth: That's not bad. Tell me more.

Ming: Well, one-bedrooms come with a bathroom, a kitchen, a fireplace in the living room, pretty big closets, and uh . . . Are you looking for a furnished or unfurnished place?

Beth: Unfurnished. I have all my own stuff. What about parking and laundry?

Ming: There's no garage. You have to park on the street. But there *is* a laundry room downstairs.

Beth: Hmm. I think I'm interested. Could you give me the address?

Ming: Sure. It's 1213 Rose Avenue. The manager's name is Mr. Azizi. Call him up or just stop by and talk to him.

Beth: Thanks, Ming. I'm going to do that tomorrow for sure.

7 Listening for Reductions page 87

A: Mr. Azizi, I have to talk to you. I have another problem.

B: Could you call me later? I'm busy now.

A: No, I need the plumber again. Could you call him right now?

B: I have a lot of things to do. I'll call him tomorrow morning, OK?

A: No, I need him right now!

B: Are you having trouble with the toilet again?

A: Yes. Look, just give me the plumber's phone number. I'll call him.

B: All right, all right. Just give me a minute and I'll do it.

9 Distinguishing Among -ed Endings

page 88

1. turned
2. rented
3. mixed
4. asked
5. recommended
6. walked
7. tested
8. followed
9. moved
10. changed

Part 2 Conversation: Touring an Apartment

3 Listening for Main Ideas page 92

4 Taking Notes on Specific Information

page 92

Mr. Azizi: So, here's the living room. Oh, and please don't touch the walls; we just painted them. I hope you like green.

Beth: Well, green is not my favorite color . . .

Mr. Azizi: As you can see, there's lots of light in here. And here's the fireplace. It's great in the winter.

Beth: Whew, it's warm in here, isn't it? Is there any air conditioning?

Mr. Azizi: No, there isn't. Just keep this window open. Oh, it's almost never this noisy.

Beth: I'm sorry, what did you say?

Mr. Azizi: Come this way. Here's your kitchen, an electric stove, a dishwasher . . . This big refrigerator is included, and there's room for a breakfast table here . . .

Beth: That's nice. Could I see the bedroom?

Mr. Azizi: Sure, it's over here. We just put in new carpeting, so . . . uh . . . we raised the rent $25.

Beth: Oh, really? Hmm . . . the bedroom looks a little small.

Mr. Azizi: But look at all the closet space! And here's the bathroom, with a shower and bathtub.

Beth: Oh, what about that leak?

Mr. Azizi: Hmm. I can't believe it. The plumber just fixed it last week.

Beth: Uh, if I decide to take this apartment, when can I move in?

Mr. Azizi: It's available on the first of the month. So that's actually the day after tomorrow.

Beth: I see. And, uh, do I have to sign . . . I mean, is there a lease?

Mr. Azizi: It's up to you. You can sign a one-year lease or you can pay month-to-month. So, uh, are you interested?

Beth: Possibly. I need to think about it a little more. And I have a few more questions.

Mr. Azizi: No problem. Let's go to my office and talk.

Part 3 Strategies for Better Listening and Speaking

Focus on Testing: Using Context Clues

page 94

Conversation 1

Sam: Alex, can I talk to you about something?

Alex: Sure, what's up?

Sam: You know, last night I couldn't study because of all the noise. And then I couldn't sleep either. You guys kept me up 'til 3:00 A.M.

Question 1: What did Alex probably do last night?

Alex: Sorry man, next time I won't have a party on a weeknight.

Conversation 2

Amy: I hate my roommate. Look at this! All the dishes are still on the table from last night! And her clothes! She never puts them in her closet. They're on the floor, on the chair, everywhere.

Susanna: Amy, why don't you talk to her about it?

Amy: I already talked to her about ten times. She won't change.

Question 2: Why does Amy hate her roommate?

Susanna: You know, you should find another roommate who isn't messy and who cleans up after herself.

Conversation 3

Tara: Do you mind if I watch the news?

Kim: Yes, actually I *do*. My favorite comedy is coming on right now.

Tara: Is that more important than the news?

Kim: Don't start that again. We had the same argument last night. Just turn to channel 4, OK?

Question 3: Which sentence is probably true?

Tara: I think our house needs another television set.

Conversation 4

Joe: Sasha, we need to pay our bills today. The telephone bill is $360 and the gas is $40.

Sasha: OK, so I'll give you $200. We're sharing everything half and half, right?

Joe: Yes, but it's not fair. *You* made most of the phone calls. And I almost never cook. So I don't want to pay half of these bills.

Sasha: But Joe, we agreed to pay everything 50–50!

Question 4: What does Joe think?

Joe: I don't think $200 is enough. This month you need to pay more than half.

Conversation 5

Carol: Alice, you know, your friends have stayed with us for over a month.

Alice: I know, but they haven't been able to find their own place to live, yet.

Carol: I understand, but we just have one bathroom, a tiny kitchen, and not much privacy.

Alice: But they're so nice—you really think there's a problem?

Carol: Yeah—we can't even relax, or watch TV, when they go to sleep on the living room floor!

Question 5: What is probably true about their apartment?

Alice: I know it's uncomfortable here for four people, but they'll leave soon, I promise.

Part 4 Real-World Tasks: Caring for Someone's House

1 Preparing to Leave Home for Vacation
page 96

Uncle: So Beth, you're sure you have time to do some things for us while we're away?

Beth: No problem. Just let me know what you need done.

Uncle: OK. First, can you get our mail from the mailbox, and any newspapers in the yard—and just put them inside the front door in a bag.

Beth: Fine. How often do you want that done?

Uncle: Every day, actually. But you'll need to feed and walk the dog twice a day, so you'll be over there anyway.

Beth: I see. What do I feed the dog, and how far should I walk him?

Uncle: A cup of dry dog food around 8:00 in the morning, and another around 5:00 should be fine. I'll leave a big bag of dog food in the kitchen. Walk him around the block when he's done eating. Oh, and keep his water bowl filled up, if you could.

Beth: Sure. Anything else?

Uncle: Well the garbage collector comes Tuesday, and I'm going to leave the garbage can down by the street today, but Tuesday night, can you put it back in the back yard for us?

Beth: I suppose so. . . .

Uncle: Oh, and can you water the rose bushes in the front yard?

Beth: How often should I do that?

Uncle: Two or three times a week if it doesn't rain . . .

Beth: So is that all?

Uncle: Just one more thing—you're welcome to enjoy the swimming pool, the house—you know we just got a giant new plasma TV—just clean up, and no wild parties, OK?

Beth: How about the keys to your BMW?

Uncle: Sorry but the car's not included. . . .

Mover: Where do you want the couch, Miss?

Beth: How about . . . here, where I'm standing.

Mover: What about the TV?

Beth: Just put it to the right side of the fireplace.

Mover: And the bookcase? You want it in the living room, too?

Beth: No—in the bedroom, please.

Mover: What about these towels?

Beth: By the bathroom door would be great.

Mover: Where should I put these boxes? They're really heavy.

Beth: Careful! Those are my dishes. Just leave them on the kitchen counter. Where are the boxes with my books?

Mover: They're next to the bed. And your clothes are there too. We put them on the bed. Is that OK?

Beth: Sure. Everything is a mess anyway.

Chapter 6 Cultures of the World

Part 1 Conversation: Learning New Customs

3 Listening for Main Ideas page 103

4 Listening for Details page 104

5 Listening for Stressed Words page 104

Kenji: So, Salma, is this your first trip to the United States?

Salma: Yes, it is.

Kenji: And what's your impression so far?

Salma: Well, the people are really friendly, and the city is beautiful. But the food; well, it's not so good.

Kenji: Oh, yeah, that's what I thought too when I first got here. But I'm used to American food now. I actually love hotdogs and French fries.

Yolanda: So last night I took Salma to a Mexican restaurant. I wanted her to try something exotic.

Kenji: Did you like it?

Salma: Yeah, the food was pretty good, but it was too much. I couldn't finish it all.

Yolanda: Salma was amazed when I took the leftovers home in a doggie bag.

Kenji: Yeah, that's funny, isn't it? They call it a doggie bag but it's for people. Anyway, what else surprised you?

Salma: That the restaurant was so cold! We don't use air conditioning so much in my country. Oh, and the water had ice in it, too. I had to put on my sweater, I was so cold!

Salma: Excuse me. Hello? [short pause] Oh, hi, Eduardo.

Waitress: Excuse me Miss, but we don't allow cell phones in the restaurant.

Salma: Oh, sorry. I didn't know . . . Eduardo, I'll have to call you back . . . That's strange for me. In Lebanon we use phones *everywhere*. I mean, we try to talk quietly in a place like this, but . . .

Kenji: Same in Japan. This kind of rule is getting more popular, though.

Yolanda: I'm sorry, Salma.

Salma: No, no, it's OK. When in Rome, do as the Romans do.

7 Listening for Reductions page 105

Anita: Well, it's time to get back to the office. I'll see you soon, Brenda.

Brenda: OK, see you . . . Wait, Anita, is this your cell phone?

Anita: Oh my goodness, yes, thanks. By the way, I almost forgot: my parents are coming for a visit next week.

Brenda: Really? I'd love to meet them.

Anita: Well, do you want to have lunch with us on Saturday?

Brenda: Saturday? Hmm . . . I promised my roommate I would go shopping with her that day. Could we get together for coffee later in the afternoon?

Anita: I don't know. They might be busy. I'll ask them and let you know.

Part 2 Lecture: Coming-of-Age Ceremonies

3 **Listening for Main Ideas** page 108

4 **Taking Notes on Specific Information** page 109

At what age does a child become an adult? The answer depends on your culture or religion. Here are a few examples.

First, in some North American Indian cultures, a boy becomes a man around the age of 13. At that time, he goes into the woods alone, without food or water, for several days. When he returns safely, he becomes an adult man. Girls become adult women as soon as they are old enough to have babies, also around the age of 12 or 13.

In the Jewish religion, children spend years studying their history and religion. Then, at age 13 for boys and 12 for girls, they go through an important religious ceremony. The boys' ceremony is called a *bar mitzvah* and the girls' is called a *bat mitzvah.* From that day, they are adults, and they are responsible for their own religious development.

In Japan today, young people become legal adults at age 20. Each year on the second Monday in January, they celebrate "Coming-of-Age Day," when all the twenty-year-olds in a town are invited to attend a special ceremony. They wear traditional clothes, listen to speeches, and visit with old friends.

Finally, in the United States, the passage into adulthood takes several years. American teenagers look forward to their 16th birthday, because in most states that is the age when they can get a driver's license. The *legal* age of adulthood is 18, when Americans can vote, get married, and work full-time.

Part 3 Strategies for Better Listening and Speaking

Focus on Testing: Using Context Clues page 112

Conversation 1

Yuka: Hi, Belinda.

Belinda: Hi, Yuka. What are you doing here?

Yuka: Oh, I was in your neighborhood. I just wanted to say hi.

Belinda: Uh, that's nice. Uh . . .

Yuka: Are you busy?

Belinda: Uh, yes, a little bit. But come in for a few minutes, anyway.

Question 1: What mistake did Yuka make?

Yuka: I'm sorry I didn't call before I came. I'll only stay a few minutes.

Conversation 2

Customer: Excuse me, waiter!

Waiter: Yes, are you ready to pay, sir?

Customer: Yes, here you are.

Waiter: Thank you. Uh . . . Excuse me, sir. Was there a problem with your food?

Customer: No. It was delicious, thank you.

Waiter: Uh, was the service OK? I mean, did I do anything. . . ?

Customer: No, you were great. Excellent service.

Waiter: Oh, OK. I just, uh, wasn't sure . . .

Question 2: What mistake did the customer probably make?

Customer: Oh, I almost forgot. Here's your tip.

Conversation 3

Woman: So how was your neighbor's party last night?

Man: Fine, but the beginning was kind of strange.

Woman: Oh? What happened?

Man: My neighbor said the party started at 8 o'clock. So I went there at exactly 8:00. I couldn't believe it: she was still in the shower, the food wasn't ready, and there were no guests.

Woman: So what did you do?

Man: Oh, I just sat down and waited for about half an hour. Then people began to arrive and the party got started.

Question 3: Who made a mistake?

Woman: I guess you didn't know: in the U.S., people never arrive at parties exactly on time.

Conversation 4

Man: Wow, this is a great house!

Woman: Thanks.

Man: When did you move in?

Woman: We bought it two months ago. We finally moved in last week.

Man: How much did you pay for it?

Woman: Uh, well, it was a good, I mean, uh, a pretty good price, uh . . . Would you like a drink or something?

Man: Yeah, a glass of water would be great, thanks.

Question 4: What mistake did the man make?

Man: It was rude of me to ask how much you paid. I'm sorry.

Conversation 5

Woman: I don't understand my new neighbors from Korea.

Man: What do you mean?

Woman: Well, yesterday was my neighbor Hyun-Ee's birthday. So I told her happy birthday and put my arms around her. You know, to give her a big hug.

Man: Uh-oh. What did she do?

Woman: She looked uncomfortable and kind of pushed me away. Don't you think that's rude?

Man: No. She probably thought *you* were rude.

Question 5: What didn't the American woman know?

Man: In Korea, it's not customary to hug people you don't know very well.

Part 4 Real-World Tasks: Dining Customs

3 Following Directions for Setting a Table page 116

Mrs. Riley: OK, so we start by putting the napkin in the center of the dinner plate, like this . . .

Ming: All right. Now what?

Mrs. Riley: Well, let's put the glasses out. Are you planning to serve wine?

Ming: Yes, of course.

Mrs. Riley: White or red?

Ming: Uh . . . does it matter?

Mrs. Riley: Well, there are different glasses for each kind of wine.

Ming: I see. Well, I plan to serve roast beef.

Mrs. Riley: In that case you'll need these glasses here. They're for red wine. But first you need to set the water glass. It goes above the plate and a little to the right. And then you put the wine glass to the right of the water glass.

Ming: Like this?

Mrs. Riley: Exactly. Now, this little plate here is for bread. You put it above the dinner plate to the left. And this is a special knife for butter. Lay it across the top of the bread plate.

Ming: All right. What's next?

Mrs. Riley: Silverware.

Ming: Sorry?

Mrs. Riley: Silverware. Knives, forks, and spoons. There are different ones for each course. Are you serving a salad?

Ming: Yes.

Mrs. Riley: And soup?

Ming: Yes.

Mrs. Riley: OK. Take this dinner knife and put it to the right of the dinner plate. Then put the soup spoon to the right of the knife. Good. Now, to the left of the plate, first put this big fork. That's the dinner fork. And put this smaller fork to the left of that. It's for salad. OK. Now, what are you serving for dessert?

Ming: Chocolate cake.

Mrs. Riley: Then you need a dessert fork. Put it above the dinner plate, with the handle pointing to the left. And then put this small spoon, for coffee, above it, with the handle pointing to the right.

Ming: All these knives and forks! How do people know which ones to use?

Mrs. Riley: Actually it's quite simple. You always use the utensil that's on the outside, and you serve the food in the same order. So, for example, you'll serve your soup first, your salad second, your main course third, and the dessert last. See?

Ming: Yes. It's really quite logical. Thanks, Mrs. Riley. You've been a great help!

Mrs. Riley: You're welcome.

Ming: Now I just have to make sure not to burn the food!

Chapter 7 Health

Part 1 Conversation: Touring a Health Club

3 **Listening for Main Ideas** page 124

4 **Listening for Details** page 124

5 **Listening for Stressed Words** page 124

Adel: Hi, I'm Adel. I'm sure you're going to like it here. Let me show you around . . . Here's the weight room. We've got the newest machines, our instructors can show you how to use them.

Peter: This is cool!

Kenji: Yeah. I really need to start lifting weights.

Adel: And here is a cardio class . . .

Peter: I've never tried cardio. It's just dancing, isn't it?

Adel: Not really. Actually, they're working harder than you think.

Kenji: And cardio is very good for your heart.

Adel: It sure is. But you should do it at least three times a week if you want to be in good shape.

Peter: Well, I already jog three times a week.

Adel: That's terrific.

Kenji: You also have boxing and yoga classes here, don't you?

Adel: Yes. I'll give you a schedule of classes when we finish our tour. Now here's our swimming pool.

Peter: Wow! Look at that woman in the middle lane. She's really fast, isn't she!

Adel: Oh, yeah. That's Ellen, one of our instructors.

Kenji: I'd like to take lessons from her!

Adel: You're not the only one. C'mon, I'll show you the showers and the locker room.

Adel: You know, if you want to join our gym, you ought to do it before the end of the month.

Kenji: Really? Why?

Adel: Well, because we have a special discount for students this month. Let's go to my office and I'll tell you all about it.

8 **Understanding Tag Questions** page 127

1. **Peter:** I've never tried cardio. It's just dancing, isn't it?
   Adel: Not really.

2. **Kenji:** You also have boxing and yoga classes here, don't you?
   Adel: Yes.

3. **Peter:** Wow! Look at that woman in the middle lane. She's really fast, isn't she?
   Adel: Oh, yeah. That's Ellen, one of our instructors.

4. **Peter:** The gym is open 24 hours a day, isn't it?
   Adel: Almost. It's open from 5 A.M. to 1 A.M.

5. **Kenji:** The pool is really crowded, isn't it?
   Peter: Yeah.

6. **Adel:** You guys are students, aren't you?
   Peter and Kenji: Yes, we are.

Part 2 A Doctor's Advice: Treating an Illness

3 **Listening for Main Ideas** page 132

4 **Taking Notes on Specific Information**
page 132

Doctor: Barbara, you're back again! What seems to be the trouble?

Barbara: Well, I woke up this morning with a terrible headache.

Doctor: Yes?

Barbara: And I had an upset stomach too. I'm feeling really weak, and my whole body feels hot, and my muscles hurt. Oh, and I'm starting to get a sore throat.

Doctor: Well, your forehead feels really warm. You probably have a fever. Let me see your throat.

Barbara: Ahhhh.

Doctor: Ah-hah. It's all red and swollen. I think you've got another case of the flu. You were sick just last month, weren't you?

Barbara: Yeah, I was.

Doctor: Are you taking good care of yourself?

Barbara: What do you mean?

Doctor: Well, do you eat right, and do you get enough sleep?

Barbara: Well, right now I'm studying for some tests and I'm very tired. I've been drinking a lot of coffee and eating pizza and hamburgers.

Doctor: You should stop drinking coffee and eat lots of fruits and vegetables. I want you to take two aspirin four times a day, drink a lot of juice, and get plenty of rest. If your throat doesn't get better in a week, I want you to call me, OK?

Barbara: So I don't need a prescription, do I?

Doctor: Not yet. Well, try to take care of yourself, and don't work too hard.

Part 3 Strategies for Better Listening and Speaking

Focus on Testing: Using Context Clues
page 135

Part 1
Conversation 1

Man: Hello, may I take your order?

Woman: Yes, I'd like a salad with low-fat cottage cheese, no dressing, please. And one slice of bread, no butter.

Man: Anything to drink?

Woman: Do you have unsweetened iced tea?

Man: Yes, we do. Will that be all, Miss?

Woman: Yes . . . oh, wait! For dessert I'll have a piece of chocolate cake with ice cream.

Question 1: What's surprising about the woman's order?

Man: You know, before you ordered that cake, I thought you were on a diet.

Conversation 2

Woman: So, that was a good workout, wasn't it?

Man: Yeah. Let's see . . . what did we do? We ran three miles, we played two sets of tennis, and we did 50 sit-ups.

Woman: Yeah. I want to get a nice cold bottle of water from the vending machine.

Man: And I want to get a bag of potato chips.

Question 2: What's surprising about what the man says?

Woman: You know, you take such good care of yourself and get so much exercise. I really don't understand why you eat junk like potato chips.

Conversation 3

Woman: Why did you wake me up?

Man: You were sleeping quite a while. I think you should cover up and get into the shade.

Woman: You think so? I really want to get a good tan.

Man: Well you already look a bit red to me.

Woman: Don't worry. I do this every summer at the beach.

Question 3: What's surprising about what the woman says?

Man: You shouldn't lie in the sun so long without protection. You're going to get a *terrible* sunburn.

Conversation 4

Man: Hi, Andrea. How're you doing?

Woman: I am so stressed out! I can't eat, I can't sleep. I feel like I'm going crazy!

Man: Why? What's the problem?

Woman: I've got so many things to do. You know, school, my job, housework, sports— there just isn't enough time for everything.

Man: You really ought to take a vacation. Maybe go to Hawaii for a week.

Woman: Oh, I don't want to do that.

Man: Why not?

Woman: It's so boring there. There's nothing to do.

Question 4: What's surprising about what Andrea said?

Man: I don't get it. You're complaining about how stressed out you are, but you don't even want some time to relax!

Part 2
Conversation 1

A: So Nancy went into the hospital last night?

B: That's right, and her husband is waiting for the news right now.

A: Is this her first?

B: Yes, so they're both very nervous. Especially Steve.

A: When can Nancy come home?

B: If all goes well, they'll both be home in a couple of days. It's exciting, isn't it?

Question 1: The situation is . . .

A: Yes, having your first baby is always very special.

Conversation 2

A: These carrots are organic.

B: What about your eggs? Are they fresh?

A: Of course. All our eggs come from local farms daily.

B: You sell vitamins, don't you?

A: Yes, they're right next to the nuts over there.

B: Your stuff looks great, but it's a little expensive.

A: Well, we sell only the best.

Question 2: The speakers are in a . . .

B: Well, I guess this is the best health food store in town.

Part 4 Real-World Tasks: Talking to Health Care Professionals

1 Taking Notes on Phone Conversations
page 138

Conversation 1

A: University Dental Clinic. May I help you?

B: Yes, I'd like to make an appointment.

A: Do you have a problem, or is it just for a checkup?

B: I think I've broken a tooth.

A: Well, can you come in tomorrow morning?

B: No, but how about after lunch?

A: Well, let me see . . . Dr. Jones can probably take you at around . . . 2:00. How's that?

B: That's great. Where is your office?

A: We're at 532 Western Avenue. That's near Third Street.

B: OK. I'll see you tomorrow at 2:00.

Conversation 2

A: Drugs R Us. May I help you?

B: Yes, I'd like to know if my prescription is ready.

A: What's the name, please?

B: Ellen Beattie.

A: Spell that, please.

B: B-E-A-T-T-I-E.

A: Oh, yes, here it is. It comes to $14.95.

B: Are there any special instructions?

A: Well, let me see. Take the pills every six hours with food. But don't worry. The instructions are also on the bottle.

B: OK. How late can I pick it up?

A: Today we're open until five o'clock.

B: All right. Thanks a lot. I'll be in later.

Conversation 3

A: Family Medicine.

B: Hi, Sherry. This is Penny Berkowitz.

A: Hi. You're bringing your baby in this afternoon, aren't you?

B: Well, our car broke down. So I'd like to change our appointment with Dr. Stork, if that's OK.

A: Sure. What's a good time for you?

B: Can I come in on Monday?

A: How about ten o'clock?

B: Fine.

A: OK. We'll see you then.

B: Oh, while we're on the phone, my husband needs a checkup. Can you take him one evening next week?

A: I think so. What about Tuesday at six o'clock with Dr. Miller?

B: That's perfect. Thanks. Bye-bye.

Chapter 8 Entertainment and the Media

Part 1 Conversation: Watching TV

3 **Listening for Main Ideas** page 145

4 **Listening for Details** page 146

5 **Listening for Stressed Words** page 146

Ming: Hey, listen to this. The average American watches four hours of TV a day.

Jack: A day? You're joking.

Ming: No, it says so right here in this newspaper. Hmm, I guess *you're* an average American, Jack. You always have your TV on.

Jack: Come on. Are you saying I'm a couch potato?

Ming: Yeah. I really think watching TV is a waste of time.

Jack: Oh, come on. Some programs are bad, like those soap operas. But what about sports or the news? You watch those sometimes, don't you?

Ming: Well, actually, for the news, I prefer the newspaper. Or the Internet.

Jack: Why?

Ming: First, because they give you a lot more information. And I can read them any time I want. Plus, I hate all the commercials.

Jack: I know what you mean. That's why, when the commercials come on, I just turn down the volume or change channels.

Ming: Yeah, I noticed that. Channel surfing drives me crazy.

Jack: OK, next time you come over, I'll let *you* have the remote control.

Ming: Oh, that's so sweet. But I have a better idea. Next time I come over, let's just turn the TV off.

7 **Listening for Reductions** page 147

A: Are you calling the movie theater?

B: Uh-huh. Don't you want to go to the movies tonight?

A: To tell you the truth, I'm pretty tired. But we can go to an early show. Do you know what you want to see?

B: Not really. I'll let you choose. *Batman III* is playing at eight and James Bond is at ten.

A: Let's see *Batman.* I'm tired now and by ten o'clock I'm going to be dead.

Part 2 News Report: An Airplane Crash

3 **Listening for Main Ideas** page 152

4 **Listening for Specific Information** page 152

Radio Announcer: Good evening. Our top story tonight: about an hour ago, a small airplane carrying six people landed safely in traffic on Highway 1. Two of the passengers received back injuries, and one of the passengers suffered a broken leg. Here's reporter Laura Jones at the scene of the crash.

Reporter: Good evening, Mark. I'm standing here on Highway 1 with two drivers who almost hit the plane as it landed. Could you tell me what you thought as you watched the plane coming down?

Witness 1: Well, at first I wasn't scared. But then I saw it was flying very low. So I drove to the side of the road in a hurry.

Reporter: And you, sir?

Witness 2: I almost didn't see the plane at all. It happened so fast. When I finally heard the plane's engine, I knew something was wrong. And then I hit my brakes. Phew . . . it was really close. I'm still shaking.

Reporter: Fortunately, no one on the ground was hurt, but the plane blocked traffic for over an hour. Officer John McNamara of the local highway police thinks the plane ran out of gasoline. A complete investigation will begin tomorrow. Back to you, Mark.

Part 3 Strategies for Better Listening and Speaking

Focus on Testing: Using Context Clues
page 154

Commercial 1

Announcer: Looking for a healthy start and a delicious flavor? Time to go to work, but no time to cook a healthy breakfast? Start your morning right with a bowl of *Flakos!*

Question 1: What are *Flakos?*

Announcer: They're my favorite cereal, and they provide all the energy I need for the morning.

Commercial 2

A: Hello?

B: Hi, Marge. Are you asleep?

A: Not anymore. Who is this?

B: It's Bill. I'm on vacation in California.

A: Bill, it's 12:00 midnight.

B: Yeah, but I have some good news! I'm calling for free! I get 5000 free night-time minutes on this new calling plan. And I got a great new camera phone!

Question 2: This is an ad for a . . .

Announcer: SureCell—the cell phone company that saves you money all day—and all night!

Commercial 3

Hi! This is Tex Lewis. I'll do anything to sell you one of these fine beauties. Lookie here.

We've got a 2005 two-door sedan here, automatic, with low mileage. This baby is clean; got new tires, GPS system, side airbags, the whole works. Take a test drive today. And it can be yours for just $16,000, or $500 per month. Come in and check it out. See you soon.

Question 3: This is an ad for . . .

Announcer: Tex's Used Cars. Quality cars for less.

Commercial 4

A: Honey, make me a sandwich.

B: Henry! It's midnight. I'm tired.

A: Honey, what's on TV?

B: I don't know. It's two o'clock in the morning.

A: Honey, can I have some breakfast?

B: Henry, it's four o'clock in the morning. Why don't you take some Dreamease?

Question 4: Dreamease is a . . .

Announcer: Dreamease, the sleeping pill that helps you get the rest you need.

Commercial 5

Man: Daisy, you must tell me everything. You believe me, don't you?

Woman: I can't, Rob. I just can't.

Man: Don't treat me this way, Daisy. I know you love me. And I love you, too.

Woman: I know. But, but I promised. And I can't break a promise.

Announcer: Her secret can destroy a life. Will she tell it? Find out this Monday at 9:00 on KNXT.

Question 5: This is an ad for a . . .

Announcer: *Daisy,* the most popular drama on television.

Part 4 Real-World Tasks: Television

2 Discussing a Program Guide page 156

Jennifer: What's on TV tonight?

Raul: Let me check the TV guide. What time is it now?

Jennifer: It's almost seven-thirty.

Raul: There are probably some game shows on.

Jennifer: Yeah, I think *Who Wants To Be a Millionaire?* is on Channel 7 at seven o'clock.

Raul: *Who Wants to Be a Millionaire?* I'm a little tired of that one.

Jennifer: OK. See if there are any good movies on.

Raul: Well, there are three movies on at eight o'clock.

Jennifer: Which ones are they?

Raul: There's *Shanghai Knights* on Channel 13—you know, the comedy with Jackie Chan.

Jennifer: I've already seen it.

Raul: Then on Channel 11 there's the *Matrix.* But you don't like science fiction, right?

Jennifer: Ugh. I hate sci-fi.

Raul: And then there's the horror movie *Scream* . . . that's on Channel 20.

Jennifer: Oh, wait—what's tonight? Wednesday? My favorite sitcom is on at eight o'clock!

Raul: At 8:00? You must be kidding—you don't want to watch *Friends* again! Channel 53 should take it off, it's so old.

Jennifer: I don't care. *Friends* is still the funniest.

Jennifer: Come on, let's make a decision.

Raul: OK. We can watch your sitcom at 8:00 if you let me watch basketball at 9:00 on channel 25.

Jennifer: Basketball? But you played basketball all afternoon!

Raul: But it's the NBA finals!

Jennifer: Fine. But I want to catch the news at 8:30. I want to know about the President's trip to Asia.

Raul: Yeah, me too. I'm sure CNN on Channel 24 will have a good report.

Jennifer: Yeah. I guess we're all set. I'll go make some popcorn.

Part 1 Conversation: Making a Date

3 **Listening for Main Ideas** page 164

4 **Listening for Details** page 164

5 **Listening for Stressed Words** page 164

Yolanda: Ming, look! I can't believe it! It's Dan. Hey! How are you?

Dan: Yolanda? Ming? Wow! I haven't seen you guys since graduation night!

Ming: I know. You look great!

Dan: Thanks. So do you!

Ming: So what have you been up to?

Dan: Well, I go to Faber College.

Yolanda: Really? Do you like it?

Dan: Yeah, so far. But I've been studying really hard.

Ming: Sure you have . . .

Yolanda: So, what's your major?

Dan: It's computer science.

Ming: Ah-h-h. That makes sense. You always *were* good at math and science.

Dan: Thanks. Anyway, what have *you* guys been up to?

Ming: Well, I'm a sales rep for a publishing company.

Dan: No kidding! How do you like that?

Ming: Oh, I love it! I'm on the road a lot, but I get to meet some interesting people.

Dan: That's terrific. And how about you, Yolanda?

Yolanda: I'm studying pre-med at State College.

Dan: Wow—you can be my doctor! You always were good at science too. Well, it was great seeing you both. Let's keep in touch from now on. E-mail me sometime. Here's my address.

1. My sister just had triplets.

2. Guess what? I'm getting married next month.

3. Would you like a job for a dollar an hour?

4. I've been dancing a lot, and I've finally learned the tango.

5. Someone hit my car yesterday. It's going to cost $1,000 to repair.

6. I met the President of the United States yesterday.

7. My sister likes to eat peanut butter and banana sandwiches.

8. I locked the keys in the car.

Part 2   Conversation: Arranging a Match

Tanya: Listen, Meena, a friend is coming to town next week. He's great looking, and I think you might enjoy going on a date. Would you like to meet him?

Meena: No thanks, Tanya. You know how traditional my family is. Dating just isn't part of our culture. In fact, I'm not supposed to go out with guys at all before marriage.

Tanya: Hmm, I see. How are you going to meet a partner, or a husband?

Meena: Oh, my family's always looking for the right kind of person. Or they might even take me to a professional matchmaker.

Tanya: Interesting . . . So what makes a good match?

Meena: Well, he's got to be from a good family from my parents' point of view. And he has to share our religious beliefs.

Tanya: That's just what *my* mother says. And. . . ?

Meena: He should be honest and hardworking, be a strong leader, but be kind.

Tanya: Sounds good to me. But what if you don't love the guy your family wants you to be with?

Meena: You know, my parents would never force me to marry someone I really couldn't accept . . . But we believe love is something that takes time—it can grow in the right situation.

Tanya: I think I understand. . . .

Meena: Maybe it doesn't sound very romantic. But our family life is really strong, and all my relatives seem pretty satisfied with their marriages.

Tanya: I wish I could say the same . . .

Part 3   Strategies for Better Listening and Speaking

Focus on Testing: Using Context Clues

Conversation 1

Man: So how long have you lived here?

Woman: I've lived here all my life. I really love it here.

Man: It seems nice, but I've been so busy with my new job and moving in to my new apartment that I haven't done any sightseeing yet. Are you free on Saturday afternoon? Maybe you could show me around a little.

Question 1: Which of these sentences is true?

Woman: Sure. Tell me, how long have you been in town?

Man: Only about three weeks.

Conversation 2

Woman: So, are you glad you left?

Man: Very glad. My salary wasn't great, as you know, and the manager was a pain in the neck.

Woman: He still is. Every day I hate going to work. But I don't know if I could find a better job.

Man: Why don't you start looking around? You might get lucky like me.

Question 2: Which of these sentences is true?

Man: I really enjoyed working with you, of course. I just didn't like the boss.

Conversation 3

Man: I've really enjoyed talking with you. Would you like to have lunch together sometime?

Woman: Thanks, you're very kind. But, well, uh, it's difficult for me to get away from work. I'm very busy.

Man: Well, how about dinner?

Woman: I'm usually too tired to go out after work.

Man: Can I call you over the weekend?

Woman: Well, this weekend my friend is coming from Miami, and I'll probably be out most of the time.

Man: How about next weekend?

Question 3: Which of these sentences is true?

Woman: Actually, I have a boyfriend, so I really can't go out with you.

Conversation 4

Man: Where's Tony?

Woman: I think he took his bike out to get some soda.

Man: Really? Do you think he can see out there? I mean it's pitch dark!

Woman: I don't know. I'm sure he's fine. It's only been about an hour.

Question 4: Which of these sentences is true?

Man: One hour! The store is just five minutes from here. I hope he's OK.

Conversation 5

Woman: Where were you? I waited forty-five minutes before I left for the party.

Man: I thought you were going to pick me up. I had to take a taxi.

Woman: Wait a minute. You said you wanted to leave your car at my house.

Man: That's *not* what I said. I said I wanted to leave my car *at home.*

Question 5: Which of these sentences is true?

Woman: Listen, I'm sorry. Let's not fight over this misunderstanding, OK?

Part 4　Real-World Tasks: Entertainment

3 Taking Notes　page 178

Call 1

Hello. This is the Fox Theater, located in the Town and Country Shopping Center. Today we're proud to present Nicole Kidman in the thrilling sci-fi film, *Invasion.* Show times for Saturday are two, six, and ten o'clock. Tickets are $10 and $5.50 for students, senior citizens, and children under 12. For more information, please hang up and call 555-0183. See you at the movies!

Call 2

Manager: Hello. Blue Note Jazz and Supper Club.

Ming: Hi. I'd like some information.

Manager: Sure, what would you like to know?

Ming: First, is there any live music tonight?

Manager: Yes, we have a terrific Brazilian singer named Bebel Gilberto. There are shows at nine and eleven.

Ming: How much is the show?

Manager: We have a $20 cover charge. But if you come for dinner, the show is free.

Ming: What's your menu like?

Manager: Our specialty is Italian food, but we serve salads and hamburgers too.

Ming: Fine. I'd like to make a reservation for two for dinner at eight, and we'll stay for the nine o'clock show. My last name's Lee—that's L-E-E.

Manager: Very good Ms. Lee, we'll see you at eight.

Call 3

You have reached the information line for Gallery Shibuya, which features live rock music nightly. The gallery is proud to present, Buffalo Daughter, now through August 6th. For show times, press 1. For directions to gallery Shibuya, press 2. For ticket information and ticket orders, press 3.

Clerk: Hi, this is Sherry speaking. Can I help you?

Ming: Yes, uh, do you still have tickets for the August 4th Buffalo Daughter show?

Clerk: How many tickets?

Ming: Two.

Clerk: I'll check.

Clerk: Yes, we have tickets for $20.00.

Ming: Is there a special price for students?

Clerk: Yes, student tickets are $8.50.

Ming: OK, that's good.

Clerk: All right, two student tickets at $8.50 each, that's $17.00. There is also a service charge of $1.00 per ticket, so your total comes to $19.00. And how would you like to pay for your tickets?

Ming: Can you hold them for me for ten minutes—I'm just a block away from you?

Clerk: I can do that—and then there's no service charge. May I have your full name please?

Ming: Ming Lee.

Clerk: Ming—M-I-N-G?

Ming: Right.

Clerk: And we need your phone number please, Ms. Lee?

Ming: 310-555-0176.

Clerk: OK, so we'll see you soon, all right? And remember to bring your student ID with you, for the student price.

Ming: Thank you very much.

Clerk: You're welcome. Bye-bye.

Ming: Bye.

Chapter 10 Sports

Part 1 Conversation: Explaining a Sport

3 Listening for Main Ideas page 183

4 Listening for Details page 184

5 Listening for Stressed Words page 184

Ming: OK guys. Let's warm up and stretch. We've got to work on balance and flexibility.

Peter: So Ming. When did you get into this Karate stuff?

Kenji: Karate's Japanese. Ming's showing us Tae Kwon Do, and it's Korean.

Peter: Cool. So, what's the difference?

Ming: Tae Kwon Do uses hundreds of different kicking moves. But Karate . . . well, Kenji, it sounds like you know something about Karate.

Kenji: Yeah—Karate uses more punches and blocks, too. Maybe you've seen guys break wooden boards with punches. You know, like . . . I learned that when I was in school.

Peter: That's great. I wish I could do that. So, Ming, why did you get into Tae Kwon Do?

Ming: I had a Korean friend in middle school and he said it could help me get in shape and build my confidence. So I tried it, and I really liked it.

Peter: It looks like you succeeded.

Ming: Well, I'm still working on it. I've really improved my speed and power. It also helps you focus—you'll see.

Peter: Awesome! Let's get started.

8 Listening for Reductions page 186

Jane: Hi Helen, Are you going out?

Helen: Yeah, I'm going to the football game. My brother's playing and I thought I'd watch him. Do you want to come?

Jane: I really can't . . . I have to study. But can you do me a favor?

Helen: OK.

Jane: Could you get me tickets for the girls' soccer game next Saturday? My cousin Sue just made the team.

Helen: Sure—that's so cool. What's her position?

Jane: I'm not sure—I'm going to call her, and I can ask her, if you want.

Helen: You don't have to—just wish her luck.

Part 2 Speech: A Female Wrestler

3 Taking Notes on Main Ideas page 189

5 Listening for Specific Information page 190

Hi, my name is Terri Whitmore. I'm 21 years old, I major in psychology, I have a boyfriend, and I love movies and shopping and cats. Yeah, most people think I'm a typical college student. That's until they find out that I'm a champion wrestler. Then of course they're surprised because in most parts of the United States and the world, the idea of women's wrestling is still new. What people don't know is that women's wrestling is growing very quickly, especially since the 2004 Olympics. That's when women's wrestling was finally included as an Olympic sport. Imagine: the sport of wrestling is one of the oldest in history, but women wrestlers couldn't compete until recently.

Anyway, people always ask me, 'Why did you choose wrestling?" Well, to me it was natural. I became interested when I was eight because my brothers were on wrestling teams. They let me participate, and I did very well. I mean I won a lot of matches and beat most of the guys. But when I turned 12, they didn't want me on the team anymore just because I was a girl. When I went to college, I started to wrestle again, this time on girls' teams.

Another thing people ask is about the rules. Are they the same as for men? Sure. Basically, the main goal in wrestling is to pin your opponent. That means you try to hold their shoulders to the floor for about one-half second. If you do that, you win right away. But there are other ways to win a match, too. You can score points; I mean points for different moves and holds. The wrestler with the most points is the winner. But you need at least three more points than the other guy. If not, then you go into overtime.

Oh, and then there are all kinds of rules about the parts of the body. You know, the parts that are OK to touch or hold, and things like that. And also, it's important to know that we compete against wrestlers in the same weight group.

Anyway, I'm really glad I chose wrestling. I like competing as an individual. In team sports, you can always blame someone else for not scoring a goal, or not catching a ball. But my success or my failure depends only on me, not on a teammate. Sure, it's a lot of pressure, but it's made me stronger and more confident.

Part 3 Strategies For Better Listening and Speaking

Focus on Testing: Using Context Clues
page 192

1. You can do this sport all year: outside in the summer and inside in the winter. You don't need any special equipment, just a bathing suit. You can do it by yourself, but you can't do it without water.

2. This sport looks like two people are fighting. They wear gloves and special protection for their teeth and sometimes for their heads. Usually men do this sport. But in the past few years, women have been participating in this sport, too.

3. This sport is not very old. It started as just a fun activity for young people who wanted to try something different from skiing. It's kind of a mix between surfing and skiing. Sometimes it's called an extreme sport, but in 1998 it became part of the Winter Olympics. Some people think this sport will be more popular than skiing in the future.

4. This sport is thousands of years old. Today it's one of the most popular Olympic events because it's very beautiful to watch. Men and women need to have great flexibility, balance and strength as they perform exercises on the floor or on special equipment.

5. This sport is a game between two teams of nine or ten players. One player throws the ball to another, who tries to hit it with a stick as far as possible. Other players use gloves to catch the ball. This sport is especially popular in North America and Japan.

Part 4 Real-World Tasks: Following Sports News

3 Sports News on the Radio page 196

Announcer Bill: And now, to Yao Lam and Kristin Fox for Faber College Weekend Sports!

Kristin: Thanks, Bill. Well it was a busy weekend in sports, wasn't it Yao?

Yao: Sure was, Kristin. Well, Faber College men's basketball lost a big game to State College, 76 to 72.

Kristin: Yeah, it was too bad—it was really close down to the last few seconds . . . On the other hand, our *women's* basketball team won their game easily. They beat Hamilton College 61 to 43.

Yao: They get stronger every game. Now turning to volleyball, the women got a rest this weekend, but the men's team played down at Washington Junior College, and they were just *unbeatable!*

Kristin: That's right—they won all three games: 21 to 15, 21 to 18 and 21 to 12. In the state college tennis tournament, we can be very proud of our own Johnson sisters.

Yao: Yeah, the twins are playing really well. Mary Johnson won her match without any trouble: 6–3, 6–2. It took her just half an hour to finish her opponent, Tina Lewis.

Kristin: Her sister Susan Johnson had to work a little harder, but also was a winner against her rival Lisa Kim. The scores for the sets were 6–4, 4–6, 7–5. It was the longest match of the day.

Yao: And finally, our women's soccer team is playing some matches on a tour down in Brazil.

Kristin: I wish I was down there reporting on that!

Yao: Me too. I understand they just finished their first game, and they almost beat the girls from College Club Rio.

Kristin: Really, what was the score?

Yao: Actually, it was a 3–3 tie—so no losers . . . well that's it, for Weekend Sports.

Kristen and Yao: Go Faber!!

Vocabulary Index

Chapter 7

aspirin
boxing
cardio
discount
eat right
fever
headache
health club
in good/bad shape
jog
lane
lift weights
locker room
ought to
prescription
rest
show (someone) around
sore throat
swim
swollen
upset stomach
weak
yoga

Chapter 8

average week
block
change channels
channel surf
couch potato
hurt
injury
land
passenger
remote control
run out of
top story
turn down the volume
turn on the TV
turn the TV off
the TV
waste of time

Chapter 9

be up to
box office
cover charge
good at
graduation
keep in touch
live music
make a reservation
make sense
on the road
pre-med
sales rep
sci-fi movie
service charge
show times
terrific
vacancy

Chapter 10

balance
beat
close
compete
confidence
flexibility
focus
get in shape
get into
individual
It was a close game.
It was a tie!
lose
loser
match
opponent
overtime
rival
score
set
stretch
tennis match
tie
warm up
What was the score?
win
winner

Skills Index

INTERACTIONS 1: LISTENING/SPEAKING AUDIO CD TRACKING INFORMATION

SILVER EDITION

Interactions 1 LISTENING/SPEAKING

Judith Tanka • Paul Most

Interactions/Mosaic Silver Edition is a fully-integrated, 18-book, academic skills series. Language proficiencies are articulated from the beginning through advanced levels <u>within</u> each of the four language skill strands. Chapter themes articulate <u>across</u> the four strands to systematically recycle content, vocabulary, and grammar.

READING	LISTENING/SPEAKING	WRITING	GRAMMAR
Mosaic 2	Mosaic 2	Mosaic 2	Mosaic 2
Mosaic 1	Mosaic 1	Mosaic 1	Mosaic 1
Interactions 2	Interactions 2	Interactions 2	Interactions 2
Interactions 1	**Interactions 1**	Interactions 1	Interactions 1
Interactions Access	Interactions Access		

NEW TO THE SILVER EDITION

- **World's most popular and comprehensive academic skills series**—thoroughly updated for today's global learners
- **All-new, full-color photo program** features a cast of engaging students participating in college life
- **Enhanced focus on listening and speaking skills, vocabulary building, test taking and critical thinking skills** promotes academic achievement
- **New strategies and activities for the TOEFL®iBT** build invaluable test taking skills
- **Online Learning Center features downloadable MP3 files** from Student Book audio program
- **New "Best Practices" approach** promotes excellence in language teaching

INTERACTIONS 1 LISTENING/SPEAKING COMPONENTS	
Teacher's Edition	0-07-329419-5
CDs	0-07-329421-7
Audiocassettes	0-07-329420-9

www.mhhe.com/interactionsmosaic

*TOEFL is a registered trademark of Educational Testing Service (ETS). This publication is not endorsed or approved by ETS.

The McGraw·Hill Companies

ISBN-13: 978-0-07-332844-7
ISBN-10: 0-07-332844-8
Part of
ISBN-13: 978-0-07-333742-5
ISBN-10: 0-07-333742-0

90000
9 780073 337425
EAN
www.mhhe.com

Mc Graw Hill McGraw-Hill